Engaging the Spirit

A Pragmatic Study of the Holy Spirit

WILLIAM "BILL" SHEA

WESTBOW
PRESS®
A DIVISION OF THOMAS NELSON
& ZONDERVAN

WestBow Press books may be ordered through booksellers or by contacting:

WestBow Press
A Division of Thomas Nelson & Zondervan
1663 Liberty Drive
Bloomington, IN 47403
www.westbowpress.com
1 (866) 928-1240

ISBN: 978-1-9736-2063-1 (sc)
ISBN: 978-1-9736-2065-5 (hc)
ISBN: 978-1-9736-2064-8 (e)

Library of Congress Control Number: 2018902265

Print information available on the last page.

WestBow Press rev. date: 02/21/2018

CONTENTS

PREFACE

I wish to thank a number of people that have encouraged me to write this brief introduction to the Holy Spirit. First, I thank my wife, Marge, who put up with all my frustration, read and reread page after page, offered gentle comments and criticisms, and through it all made this a better book. Second, I want to thank the "Survivors" Sunday school class at University Christian Church for letting me bounce ideas off of them and helping me find all those places that were unclear or just plain incoherent. Third, I thank Bill and Ione Parschall for first suggesting I write the book. Without their love of God and interest in the Holy Spirit, I may not have had the courage to even attempt this writing.

It goes without saying that I thank the Holy Spirit, who lives within me, guides me, and encourages me. My fervent prayer is that all who read this will be drawn closer to God, Christ, and the Holy Spirit.

INTRODUCTION

As I entered into this meager attempt at taking on such an enormous task as a study of the Holy Spirit, I was initially overwhelmed. Who was I to take on this task when there were so few that had made this attempt before me? Immediately, the thought struck me; I am a possessor of the Spirit. I have both the Word of God and all of history to show who the Holy Spirit is and what He does.

This left me with one other question: Can I put into words what I know in my mind and feel in my heart in such a way that others can benefit from my knowledge and experiences? The reader will be responsible for answering that question for him- or herself.

Before we start this study, it is important to understand why we are doing this. Why bother to study the Holy Spirit? Of what difference does it make whether or not we know anything about the Spirit? If we are simply doing this for an intellectual exercise, it is probably a waste of time; however, if our true purpose is to understand the Holy Spirit and how He works in our lives, I believe His power and influence will grow within each of us, and, ultimately, we will bring glory to God.

WHY STUDY THE HOLY SPIRIT?

It was a warm July day when we got out of church and were standing in the parking lot visiting. Our Sunday school class had been missing Bill the past several Sundays. I noticed Ione, Bill's wife standing beside the car waiting for him to come out of church. She and I started talking. "Tell Bill we've missed him lately," I said. She paused and replied that Bill had been doing his own Bible study at home lately.

Just about that time Bill strolled up, and the conversation switched to what Bill was studying at home. "It's the Holy Spirit," he said. As we continued to talk, he commented on how seldom we hear anything about the Holy Spirit. We have sermons and Sunday school lessons on just about everything, but seldom do we speak about the Spirit. Later that day, while sitting at home, I mentioned to my wife, Marge, that I wondered if our next study in Sunday school ought to be about the Holy Spirit.

After much prayer, I embarked on this study. My hope is that this will prove beneficial to all those who struggle through their Christian lives never knowing the power, love, guidance, and strength of the Holy Spirit.

Each of us in our lifetimes has run into people in one of several categories: they have never heard of the Holy Spirit; or they have heard but don't believe; or they have heard and believe but have only a vague understanding of what and why they believe; and finally, a few have heard, believe, and know why they believe. It might behoove each of us to ask ourselves in which of these categories we belong.

After being immersed in Christian baptism at the age of twelve, I found myself in the category of believing but not sure what I believed or why. I found myself as the apostle Paul wrote to the church in Ephesus: "Tossed here and there by waves and carried about by every wind of doctrine, by the trickery of men, by craftiness in deceitful scheming" (Eph. 4:14 NASB). I did not know for sure what or even why I believed in the Holy Spirit; I was easily convinced by any logical-sounding argument that came along.

Most of my Christian friends in those days were no different from me. We considered that if there was a devil (an unholy spirit), then it seemed reasonable that there was a Holy Spirit to serve as a counterbalance. Although at that time, I do not believe that I had thought it through quite as clearly as that.

The question we started with was, "Why study the Holy Spirit?" It seems reasonable to me that if we believe there is a Holy Spirit, then we ought to know something about it, Him, or whatever.

In the next several chapters, we are going to consider a number of different things. For example, is the Holy Spirit a person or a thing? Scripture says, "But Stephen, full of the Holy Spirit" (Acts 7:55). What does it mean to be "full of the Holy Spirit"? Or how about this: "The Spirit said to Philip, 'Go to that chariot ... '" (Acts 8:29). Can a spirit really talk to us?

I am convinced that by studying the teachings in the New Testament, we can find the answers to all our questions. The men who wrote the New Testament were men who had, largely, spent time with Jesus and experienced the power of the Holy Spirit working in their own lives. By studying what they had to say about the Holy Spirit, we will not only have a better understanding of the Holy Spirit, but also we can have richer, fuller, more satisfying lives, and we can fulfill God's plan for our lives.

CHAPTER 1

Understanding the Trinity

Before we begin our study of the Holy Spirit, we must consider who or what the Holy Spirit is. He is a part of the Holy Trinity. Now, you will not find the word *trinity* in the Bible if you look for it. It is not there. It is a conceptual understanding of who God is.

When one first opens the Word of God and turns to the first chapter of the first book, Genesis, and reads the first two verses, he or she is immediately confronted with the Holy Spirit. For these first two verses read, "In the beginning God created the heavens and the earth. And the earth was formless and void, and darkness was over the surface of the deep; and the *Spirit of God* was moving over the surface of the waters" (Gen. 1:1–2 NASB; my emphasis). Here we have the introduction of the Holy Spirit moving over the surface of the waters. Throughout the Old Testament, we will find the Spirit of God being referred to by a variety of terms, such as the Spirit of the Lord. The New Testament will generally use the name Holy Spirit. In Genesis 1:26, the phrase "then God said, 'Let *us* make man in *our* image'" (emphasis mine) references for the first time the multiplicity of God. This is referred to as the Trinity and will be discussed later.

Only in the Holy Word of God do we find the attestation of both the Godhead and personality of the Holy Spirit. It is interesting to note that in the beginning, Genesis 2:19, Adam is called upon to give names to all God had created, but he does not give a name to God. God Himself has revealed to us who He is. No mortal person has ever been called to give a name to God.

The second part of the Godhead is God the Son, Jesus. Some people assume since Jesus referred to God as father, that meant the same relationship we humans have. However, in the scriptures, human relationships begin with a father giving birth to a child. The Greek term is GENNAO, meaning the male role in the producing of offspring, or to beget, or procreate. In the gospels, mention is made of Mary's pregnancy, but the term GENNAO is not used. The gospels shift from her pregnancy to the birth without any human intervention. The apostle Paul references this in his letter to the Philippian church: "Although he was in the form of God and equal with God, he did not take advantage of this equality. Instead, he emptied himself by taking on the form of a servant, by becoming like other humans, by having a human appearance. He humbled himself by becoming obedient to the point of death, death on a cross" (Phil. 2:6–8 GW). No mention is made of Jesus having a father involved in the procreation process. Like God, Jesus was, is, and always will be.

Jesus is the incarnation of God. He is God in human form. Some say He is God with skin on. The apostle John begins his gospel, "In the beginning was the Word, and the Word was with God, and the Word was God. He was with God in the beginning" (John 1:1–2). Jesus attested to the fact of the Godhead when He said, "Believe me that I am in the Father and the Father is in me" (John 14:11).

The third part of the Trinity is the Holy Spirit. We find a clear statement to this effect written by the apostle Paul to the church at Corinth: "My message and my preaching were not with wise and persuasive words, but with a demonstration of the Spirit's power, so that your faith might not rest on men's wisdom, but on God's power" (1 Cor. 2:4–5). Then, a little way further, he wrote, "The Spirit searches all things, even the deep things of God. For who among men knows the thoughts of a man except the man's spirit within him? In the same way, no one knows the thoughts of God except the Spirit of God" (1 Cor. 2:10b–11).

We need to understand there is an absolute equality between the three persons of the Godhead. There is no difference in exaltation or importance. Some claim that since the Son is the manifestation of the Father, He is somehow inferior to the Father. This is false! The same group claims that since the Spirit is sent from the Father and the Son, He is of lesser importance than the Father and the Son. This is also false! The full name of the Godhead is Father, Son, and Holy Spirit. This has resulted in a number of confessions and creeds.[1] The order of pronouncement makes no difference. You can place the three in any order since all three are equal. God the Holy Spirit, God the Son, and God the Father is the same as God the Son, God the Father, and God the Holy Spirit.

HE, SHE, OR IT?

Currently, gender is a volatile social and moral issue. We are dealing socially with such things as same-sex marriage and the morality of transgenderism. We have become confused by something that was so clearly understood throughout the ages. Until our day, there were two genders, male and female.

At this time, Facebook lists five different genders, and fifty-eight variants of those five genders have turned up. The Bible simply states that God created man and that He created woman from man. Period, end of story! Only the audacity of humans attempting to justify their own sins could lead us so far astray from this simple truth.

---

[1] An example is the Westminster Confession (II, III): "In the unity of the Godhead there be three Person of one substance, power, and eternity: God the Father, God the Son, and God the Holy Ghost." In support of this confession, we have several biblical statements: "Therefore, go and teach all nations, baptizing them in the name of the Father, and of the Son, and of the Holy Ghost" (Matt. 28:19), and "May the grace of the Lord Jesus Christ, and the love of God, and the fellowship of the Holy Spirit be with you all" (2 Cor. 13:14).

So is the Holy Spirit male or female, or simply a thing, an "it"? Virtually every reference to the Holy Spirit in the Bible uses the male pronoun *he*. The feminist movement of the sixties claimed that God was a woman. This never really got much traction. Psychologically we understand that if you say something often enough, loud enough, and long enough, people will begin to believe what you say is true whether there is a shred of truth in it or not. That is the foundation of politics. However, the only real source for understanding the gender of the Holy Spirit must come from the Spirit Himself. In John's gospel, John writes that Jesus said, "But the counselor, the Holy Spirit, whom the Father will send in my name, he will teach you all things and remind you of everything" (John 14:26). If we believe the doctrine of the Trinity, that God is three persons, Father, Son, and Holy Spirit, then we must accept the fact that the Holy Spirit is a being, not a thing. There are only two genders of beings, male and female, and Jesus, the Son, uses the male reference when speaking of the Holy Spirit, so it only seems logical that the Holy Spirit is a male being.

CHAPTER 2

The Functions of the Spirit

Bob finally showed up. I had been waiting on him to go to a meeting. "What took you so long?" I asked.

"I was waiting on the Spirit to show me which tie I should wear," he responded.

At the time I thought that was silly, but now I realize how serious he was. Some people take their relationship with the Spirit very seriously, while most do not take that relationship seriously enough. Bob believed that the Holy Spirit guided him in every decision he made, regardless of how minute it was.

Just what is the job of the Holy Spirit? Is it to hold our hands through each and every moment of life? Jesus said, "I will ask the Father, and he will give you another Counselor to be with you forever—the Spirit of truth. The world cannot accept him, because it neither sees him nor knows him. But you know him, for he lives with you and will be in you" (John 14:16). In another place Jesus said, "But the Counselor, the Holy Spirit, whom the Father will send in my name, will teach you all things and will remind you of everything I have said to you" (John 14:26). And again, Jesus said, "When he [Holy Spirit] comes, he will convict the world of guilt in regard to sin and righteousness and judgment" (John 16:8). Each of these passages gives us an idea of the Spirit's functions. They generally fall into four basic areas: to counsel or advocate, to guide, to testify, and to convict. Let us look at each of these in detail.

COUNSEL (ADVOCATE)

A night that was supposed to be filled with joy had turned into a night of confusion and sorrow. Passover was a time the Jews remembered how God had rescued them from slavery in Egypt. This was the greatest celebration of the year. Jesus had just finished washing the disciples' feet, and they did not understand why He had done that. Surely, it was they who should be washing His feet; after all, He was the Teacher, not them.

After they sat down to eat, Jesus said, "'I tell you the truth, one of you will betray me.' They were very sad and began to say to him one after another, 'Surely not I, Lord?'" (Matt. 26:21–22).

It did not stop there. Next Jesus told them He was going to leave them! "Where I'm going, you cannot follow now, but you will follow later," He said. Peter was indignant and asked, "Lord, why can't I follow you now? I will lay down my life for you." At this, Jesus told him that he would deny Him three times before the rooster crowed (Matt. 26:31–35).

Then Jesus told them, "I will pray to the Father, and he will give you another Counselor[2] to be with you forever" (John 14:16). Knowing their sorrow, Jesus promises to send the Holy Spirit to take His place in the world. Another meaning of the term *paraclete* is "one who stands alongside." One of the pictures of the Holy Spirit is that of a defense lawyer standing beside his client in a court of law. Just as the lawyer guides his client through the morass of legality, counseling, and offering comfort in times of extreme difficulty, the Holy Spirit guides us through the morass of life, offering His counsel and comfort as we strive to serve God.

How many times have you found that in a moment of deep

---

[2] The Greek word is *paraclete*, meaning helper, counselor, advocate, comforter. The literal translation is "together make strong."

sorrow and suffering you have heard that still, small voice saying, "I am the one sent by the Father to be with you"? Too often, we try to rely on our own strength to get through tough times when if we truly trusted God's Word we would know that He will never forsake us but will walk alongside of us giving us comfort and confidence that cannot come from any other source.

Early in my ministry, while serving as a Riley County, Kansas, police chaplain, I was often called on to deliver death notifications to the next of kin.

On one particular occasion, the phone rang around 2:00 a.m. on a Sunday. An army warrant officer, who had recently moved to our area, was killed in a one-car accident. He was en route from Wichita and was within two miles of home when the accident happened. I was to make the death notification. I decided to take my own car in case the officer who would be with me received a call and had to leave.

All the way to the house I prayed, "What am I to say to the wife who waited at home? Were there children at the house who just lost a father? Did the family have any close friends in the area? Lord, help me!"

We arrived at the house and immediately noticed the interior lights were still on. I rang the doorbell. A young woman in her late twenties hesitantly answered the door. Her face showed the concern that was in her heart. When she saw the police officer, she gasped, and her face turned pale. After introducing myself, I asked if we could step inside.

The house was vacant of all but a small table and chairs in the kitchen. A portable television sat on the kitchen counter. Their household goods had not yet arrived from their previous duty station. She was alone and knew no one in the area. After notifying her sister in Kansas City, we began to talk.

While waiting for her sister to arrive, I did my best to comfort her. She was a believer, of sorts. During the course of the morning, the Holy Spirit guided my thoughts and speech as only the Spirit can. By the time her sister arrived, I had only enough time to drive to the church for our morning services. I do not remember the sermon that morning, only that it wasn't what I had prepared. The only thing that got me through that morning was the Spirit's comfort and counsel, testifying through me.

I believe that God spoke to her through me. It was not my knowledge, preparation, or theological studies that guided my thoughts: It was the Holy Spirit Himself who spoke through me. The Spirit provided comfort to her as He spoke through me to testify about Jesus Christ and how He is with us and gives us comfort and peace in times of grieving.

MINISTRY (WORKING FOR US AND THROUGH US)

The second function of the Spirit is to work. We find from the very beginning of time the Holy Spirit was actively working. The very first page of the Bible starts, "In the beginning God created the heavens and the earth. The earth was without form and void, and darkness was upon the face of the deep; *and the Spirit of God* was moving over the face of the waters" (Gen. 1:2 RSV; emphasis mine).

So, here is the Holy Spirit at the very beginning of time performing one of the basic functions God requires of Him. When we find the people of God fulfilling God's will, we find the Holy Spirit is actively involved in it. Consider for a moment Gideon, the son of Joash. In Judges 6:25–10:2, the Lord told Gideon to pull down an altar built to worship Baal. Gideon did as the Lord told him, but he did it at night because he was afraid of what his family and the men of the town might do to him.

The next day, the men of the town found the altar had been torn down, and they were furious! They concluded it was Gideon who did it and came to get him and put him to death. But, Joash, Gideon's father, stood up for him and asked the townspeople who among them would stand up and fight for Baal? Or would they let Baal stand up and fight for himself. Not willing to let Baal handle things, a number of different tribes joined forces against Gideon with the intent on destroying him, but God didn't leave Gideon to his own strength, "Then the Spirit of the LORD came upon Gideon, and he blew a trumpet, summoning the Abiezrites to follow him" (Judg. 6:34). Even though the Spirit of the Lord (i.e., the Holy Spirit) had come upon him, Gideon was not convinced that he could defeat the opposing force. So he put God to the test! We remember the story of Gideon and the fleece. Three times Gideon laid out a fleece to test God, and each time God passed the test (Judg. 6:36–39). To make sure Gideon did not rely on his own strength in battle, God pared down the army of Gideon from thirty-two thousand men to ten thousand men, then from ten thousand to just three hundred men (Judg. 7:1–8)!

If we keep reading, we find God (the Holy Spirit) guiding Gideon, and Gideon defeats all the bad guys. The point is that when God wants us to do something for Him, He does not leave us hanging out by ourselves, but His Spirit fills us to make sure we can accomplish all that He would have us accomplish. Too often I have had people say to me that they believed God was calling them to do something, but they didn't feel capable or comfortable in doing it. The Holy Spirit ministering through us is not a matter of feeling; rather, it is a matter of trust and faith.

What would have happened if Joan of Arc had trusted her feelings and not trusted in the Holy Spirit? Joan was born in Domrémy, a village which was then in the French part of the duchy of Bar. She was the daughter of a pious, poor peasant farmer. She stated, during personal testimony at her trial in 1425, that she had her first vision at the age of thirteen. She claimed to have been told to drive out the English who had seized the land and driven out many of her neighbors, and bring the dauphin[3] to Reims for his coronation. At the age of sixteen, Joan insisted on going to the royal court at Chinon. According to witnesses, she stated, "I must be at the King's side ... there will be no help (for the kingdom) if not from me. Although I would rather have remained spinning [wool]

---

[3] Dauphin was the title given to the heir apparent to the throne of France from 1350 to 1791.

at my mother's side … yet must I go and must I do this thing, for my Lord wills that I do so."[4] She was able to convince Charles VII to let her lead an army against the English at Orleans in 1429. This coincided with the first French victory against the English since the defeat at Agincourt in 1415. Joan was able to turn a political war into a religious war by claiming the divine nature of her mission. "After years of one humiliating defeat after another, both the military and civil leadership of France were demoralized and discredited. When the Dauphin Charles granted Joan's urgent request to be equipped for war and placed at the head of his army, his decision must have been based in large part on the knowledge that every orthodox, every rational option had been tried and had failed. Only a regime in the final straits of desperation would pay any heed to an illiterate farm girl who claimed that the voice of God was instructing her to take charge of her country's army and lead it to victory."[5] In the spring of 1430 Joan was thrown from her horse and taken captive by the English. In the trial that followed, Joan was ordered to answer to some seventy charges against her, including witchcraft, heresy, and dressing like a man. On the morning of May 30, 1431, at the age of nineteen, Joan was taken to the old marketplace of Rouen and burned at the stake. Her fame only increased after her death, however, and twenty years later a new trial ordered by Charles VII cleared her name.

Throughout history, we have heard of God's people doing things that people considered impossible, but for one who is filled with God's Spirit, nothing is impossible.

TESTIFY (TELLING THE TRUTH ABOUT JESUS)

The third basic function of the Holy Spirit is to testify. He testifies to the truth about Jesus Christ. Many Christians have had the experience of speaking with someone when the topic changes

---

[4] Pernoud, *Joan of Arc by Herself and Her Witnesses*, 35.
[5] http://www.stjoan-center.com/military/stephenr.html.

to religion. What church do you attend? Why do you go there? Or maybe it starts while trying to comfort someone who is experiencing grief in their own life and you begin to share with him or her about how you got through a period of grief in your own life. All of a sudden you find the Spirit prompting you to share how having Jesus in your life makes all the difference in the world. The Spirit might even encourage you with what to say, even when you have no idea what to say. Christ himself promised this: "When the [paraclete] Helper comes, whom I will send to you from the Father, *that is* the Spirit of truth who proceeds from the Father, He will testify about Me" (John 15:26 NASB).

Again,

> I have many more things to say to you, but you cannot bear *them* now. But when He, the Spirit of truth, comes, He will guide you into all the truth; for He will not speak on His own initiative, but whatever He hears, He will speak; and He will disclose to you what is to come. He will glorify Me, for He will take of Mine and will disclose *it* to you. All things that the Father has are Mine; therefore, I said that He takes of Mine and will disclose *it* to you. (John 16:12–15 NASB)

Now in our scientific world, this is a hard concept to accept. We have been taught that if you cannot see it, touch it, or taste it, it does not exist. So how can something that does not exist help us when we need it? That is just the point; we accept Christ by faith and believe in Him. We must also accept by faith that the Holy Spirit, whom Christ has sent to us, dwells within us and testifies to the truth about Christ.

We are not the only ones to have this problem. Consider Peter and John following Christ's ascension to heaven (Act 3:1–4:31). They were in the temple courts and healed a man crippled from birth. Peter and John refused to accept credit for what had happened and began to testify about Jesus and God. While they were still speaking, the priests and the captain of the temple guard along with other religious men came to them complaining because they were teaching the people about Jesus and resurrection from the dead. "The priests and the captain of the temple guard and the Sadducees came up to Peter and John while they were speaking to the people. They were greatly disturbed because the apostles were teaching the people and proclaiming in Jesus the resurrection of the dead" (Acts 4:1–2). They threw Peter and John in jail!

The next day, the high priest and other high-ranking elders interrogated Peter and John concerning the healing. Now take note of this: "Then Peter, *filled with the Holy Spirit*, said to them …" (verse 8; emphasis mine). Here we see the Holy Spirit filling Peter and John that they might testify to the truth of Jesus Christ. Another thing we might take note of is that when they had initially spoken to the crowd about Jesus, the scriptures say that many believed.

CONVICT (CONVINCE OF SINFULNESS)

The fourth function of the Holy Spirit is to convict. This has been for me and many others I know an obstacle in our ministries. We feel that when we testify about Jesus, if the person(s) we are testifying to does not accept Jesus, it is somehow our fault. The truth is that we are called to testify, but the Holy Spirit is the one who *convicts* others of the truth in order that they might believe.

Listen to what Jesus said about this: "But I tell you the truth: It is for your good that I am going away. Unless I go away, the Counselor will not come to you; but if I go, I will send him to you. When he comes, *he will convict the world of guilt* in regard to sin and righteousness and judgment" (John 16:7–8 NIV; emphasis mine). He, that is the Holy Spirit, the Comforter, the Counselor, will convict the world. It is not our responsibility to do what Jesus Himself said was the Holy Spirit's job.

A number of years ago while living in Decatur, Georgia, and

attending the Peachcrest Christian Church, I would go out most every Monday evening with the pastor, Steve Graham, and call on visitors to the church. There was one particular couple we had visited with several times and shared the gospel. The wife was a believer, but the husband was not.

After each visit, I felt a twang of guilt that we had failed to convince the young man of the truth of scripture. I had heard several evangelists talk about the number of people who had come to the Lord through their testimony. Yet, Steve and I both had done everything in our power to convince this young man, to no avail. What were we doing wrong? It was not that we were not sincere enough. It was not for a lack of trying, yet nothing seemed to work.

One evening while visiting with the same young man, Steve asked him, "Would you like accept Jesus Christ as your Lord and Savior"? Much to our surprise, he responded with a less than enthusiastic yes.

Steve and I arranged to baptize him the following Sunday. He showed up as promised, along with several family members. Following the morning worship service, Steve immersed the young man in Christian baptism. Unfortunately, that was the last time Steve or I saw him.

Now I relate this story to say I am not convinced that the young man was ever convicted by the Holy Spirit. I wonder if he gave in so he could say, "Now get off my back!" Maybe Steve and I both were so convinced that it was our job to convict the young man that we drove him to desperation.

If we remember that our job is to testify, not to convict, maybe we would be more willing to do our job. Having taught personal evangelism for a number of years, I have witnessed a general fear of failure on the part of many believers. They were more than willing to "ride shotgun" as long as they were not responsible for someone else's soul. No matter how many times I said, "They are rejecting Christ, not you," or, "Just share the truth and let the Holy Spirit do the convicting," there was still a genuine fear that prevented them from testifying about Christ. In a later chapter, we will look at another reason for that fear, and that is the unholy spirit.

The convicting, or convincing, ministry of the Holy Spirit is threefold—of sin, of righteousness, and of judgment.

1. Of Sin. Before one can repent and seek forgiveness, he or she must recognize the fact that he or she is a sinner. Some discount sin, believing that morality is a religious thing, and they are not concerned with that. These same people often believe that in the end, there is either nothing, or if heaven exists, they will go to heaven, since they have lived fairly good lives. The truth is, according to Romans 3:23: "For all have sinned and fall short of the glory of God," and in Romans 6:23: "The wages of sin is death."

What difference is there between one who reads the scriptures and desires to be saved from the penalty of his or her sin and one who chooses to ignore it? That difference is the conviction of the Holy Spirit. John McArthur[6] states, "Among the most hotly contested and persistent debates in the history of the confessing church, the doctrine of election is perhaps the greatest of all. The question goes like this: Does God choose sinners to be saved and then provide for their salvation? Or, does God provide the way of salvation that sinners must choose for themselves?"[7]

The doctrine of election is a topic far too intense for our purpose at this time. So the question for us is, "What role does the Holy Spirit play in salvation?" Whether God elects us ahead of time, or we choose to accept Christ's atoning death on the cross, it is through the convicting of the Holy Spirit that we ultimately acknowledge our sin, repent, and are baptized.

---

[6] John Fullerton MacArthur Jr. (born June 19, 1939) is an American pastor and author known for his internationally syndicated radio program *Grace to You*.

[7] John McArthur, *Is the Doctrine of Election Biblical?* http://www.gty.org/resources/Articles/A191/Is-the-Doctrine-of-Election-Biblical.

2. Of Righteousness. This is a biblical truth issue. Once we have been convicted of our sin, repented, and then been baptized, we must accept the fact that we are now righteous or have received God's approval. It is not that we have done something to make that claim; rather, it is God who makes the claim: "But now a righteousness from God, apart from law, has been made known, to which the Law and the Prophets testify. *This righteousness from God comes through faith in Jesus Christ to all who believe.* There is no difference, for all have sinned and fallen short of the glory of God and are justified freely by his grace through the redemption that came by Christ Jesus" (Rom. 3:21–24; emphasis mine). It is God who both justifies us and declares us righteous when we come to believe in Jesus Christ. "God had Christ who was sinless, take our sin, so that we might receive God's approval through Him" (2 Cor. 5:21 GW). We are God's righteousness, and this is not because of anything we have done other than accept what God has offered to us through faith in Jesus!

So what does it mean to be righteous? Fundamentally, it means having God's approval. It should be understood that there are two parts to righteousness: a permanent part, which is being in a right relationship with God (this is the part that comes through faith in Jesus Christ), and a changing part, which is most often impacted by changing social conditions.[8] This changing part is the aspect of man that wants to do what is right in the sight of God, but is constantly being influenced by the surrounding culture. This has caused considerable differences in church doctrine today. A good example of this is the homosexual issue. Most evangelical congregations are not willing to accept openly gay individuals or couples into membership in the church. On the other hand, most mainline denominations are just the opposite. Both groups claim to be following biblical teaching; one on the side of obedience and the other on the side

---

[8] http://www.internationalstandardbible.com/R/righteousness.html.

of compassion. Whichever position one takes, however, it must be understood that the changeable part of righteousness does not affect the permanent part.

3. Of Judgment. The belief in God's judgment of humanity is an important aspect of Christianity, as it is in Judaism, Islam, and most of the world's other religions. In the Old Testament, we find God's judgment of the unfaithful in the form of natural disasters, such as floods and famines. The rewards for the righteous were plentiful crops and livestock. They were also blessed with many children, especially sons, which were important for ongoing line of descendants, as well as workers in an agrarian society.

In the New Testament, however, we find a different focus on judgment. Here, judgment is focused on Satan, or the devil, as opposed to humanity. John probably said it best when he stated, "The reason the Son of God appeared was to destroy the devil's work" (1 John 3:8). When Jesus sent out the twelve disciples, He, "gave them power and authority to drive out all demons and to cure diseases, and he sent them out to preach the kingdom of God and to heal the sick."

1. Judgment is for all, both the "living and the dead" (Acts 10:42), both Christian and non-Christian (Rom. 14:10–12). John the Baptist remarked that the final judgment of God is imminent and cannot be avoided (Matt. 3:7–10). It is associated with the final days, and Jesus is to be the judge (1 Cor. 4:5; 2 Thess. 1:5–10).

2. Judgment includes the idea of reward and punishment. Jesus said, "Rejoice and be glad, because great is your reward in heaven, for in the same way they persecuted the prophets who were before you" (Matt. 5:12); "For the Son of Man is going to come in his Father's glory with his angels, and then he will reward each person according to what he has done"

(Matt. 16:27). However, for the unrighteous, punishment will be severe: "Then he will say to those on his left, 'Depart from me, you who are cursed, into the eternal fire prepared for the devil and his angels'" (Matt. 25:14). God said, "But the cowardly, the unbelieving, the vile, the murderers, the sexually immoral, those who practice magic arts, the idolaters and all liars—their place will be in the fiery lake of burning sulfur'" (Rev. 21:8).

The concept of reward and punishment is not to be confused with one's personal salvation. We do not earn our salvation through "works." The apostle Paul clearly states, "For it is by grace you have been saved, through faith—and this not from yourselves, it is the gift of God—not by works, so that no one can boast" (Eph. 2:8–9). "In the final judgement, a person's work will be the evidence of whether a living faith is present in him or not."[9]

We cannot leave this thought without touching on a related question. "Does God bless in tangible ways today those who strive to live lives of faithfulness?" Since I do not believe in coincidence or luck in life, I must assume that God is in control. However, if I believe it is God's desire that we enjoy all He has created for our well-being, how can I explain why bad things happen to good people?

Have you ever prayed for healing for a friend, and the person was not healed? I believe most Christians have. How do we explain that? Have you ever known a good Christian family that suffered some extremely devastating mishap? Were they being punished for some unknown sin? While we can never answer these questions, we still see evidence of righteous followers of the Lord being blessed on a regular basis. Part of this is what we call "cause and effect." If I'm doing drugs, living a promiscuous lifestyle, or consuming alcohol excessively, I can expect bad things to happen. On the other hand, if I am living a Christian lifestyle and doing what is right, I can anticipate avoiding bad things.

---

[9] Ferguson and Wright, *New Dictionary of Theology*, 358.

While good things happen to bad people and bad things happen to good people, we still see God blessing His people today.

3. Final judgment will be the conclusion of all life, as we know it. It will be the separation of the righteous and the unrighteous. Scripture teaches that at the time of God's choosing, those who have accepted Christ as both Lord and Savior will be saved and spend eternity with God in Heaven. ("Yet to all who received him, to those who believed in his name, he gave the right to become children of God— children born not of natural descent, nor of human decision or a husband's will, but born of God" (John 1:12–13); "For God so loved the world that he gave his one and only Son, that whoever believes in him shall not perish but have eternal life" (John 3:16); "God made him who had no sin to be sin for us, so that in him we might become the righteousness of God" (2 Cor. 5:21).

Salvation can only come by a clear choice. All men have sinned and are deserving of eternal damnation (Rom. 3:23, 6:23), but the door to salvation is Christ: "Here I am! I stand at the door and knock. If anyone hears my voice and opens the door, I will come in and eat with him, and he with me" (Rev. 3:20). This choice is of immediate importance! One cannot wait until he or she lies at death's door. There is no proof in scripture that simply praying the "believer's prayer" in the moments before death overcomes a lifetime of disobedience. The requirements for salvation are simple: believe, confess, repent, be baptized, and live faithful lives.[10] What scripture does promise is that when we have fulfilled these actions, we can be sure, without a doubt, of our salvation.

---

[10] For more information on this topic, refer to chapter 3.

What Can the Christian Expect from the Holy Spirit?

HE GIVES LIFE

While there are a number of things the Christian can expect to receive from his association with the Holy Spirit, there is none as great as the mere fact that the Holy Spirit gives life to the Christian. In the gospel of John, chapter 6, John tells of Jesus with a group of his disciples. He is explaining to them that they must "eat of his flesh" and "drink of his blood" if they were to be raised up "at the last day." He then says to them, "The Spirit gives life; the flesh counts for nothing. The words I have spoken to you are Spirit and they are life" (John 6:63). The apostle Paul commented on this in his letter to the church at Rome: "And if the Spirit of him who raised Jesus from the dead is living in you, he who raised Christ from the dead will also give life to your mortal bodies through his Spirit, who lives in you" (Rom. 8:11). We need to note that in the following years there were those who claimed that Christians were cannibals based on these writings.

How should we understand this today? Scripture teaches that one can only receive salvation by accepting the facts that (1) Jesus is the Son of God, (2) that He took the sins of the world upon His shoulders at the cross upon which He died, and (3) that He died, was buried, was resurrected on the third day, and ascended into heaven. Upon accepting these facts, one repents of his or her sins, is baptized into Christ, and lives a faithful life. We learn these things as we read the biblical accounts of the life and death of Christ in the New Testament.

At this point let me make a comprehensive statement, which we will break down and examine piece by piece; when we repent of our sins, ask Jesus to be our Lord and Savior, and are baptized, we receive the Holy Spirit into our own bodies. This is referred to as the "indwelling of the Holy Spirit" and is necessary in order for us to receive salvation. This is not to be confused with the "filling of the Spirit," which we will discuss later.

The first part of this statement has to do with repentance. The Greek word for repentance is METANOIA and means, literally, to turn around and go the opposite direction. When we repent of our sins, we recognize that we are sinning, and we stop and do all in our power not to commit those sins again. This involves a change of heart about the things we do. The apostles, following the receiving of the Holy Spirit themselves, began to testify openly about Jesus. We find a record of Peter's testimony in the book of Acts, chapter 2. After hearing what he had to say, the crowd cried out, "What must we do to be saved?" Peter responded, "Repent and be baptized, every one of you, in the name of Jesus Christ for the forgiveness of your sins. And you will receive the gift of the Holy Spirit" (Acts 2:38).

Some people will claim to repent and seek forgiveness after they have done something wrong, but this is prompted by the fact that they feel sorry they got caught at what they were doing, not that they were sorry for what they did. This is not true repentance.

True repentance is prompted by what is known as "godly sorrow."[11] One of the best-known biblical examples of this is in the story of the prodigal son. This story tells of a young man who takes his inheritance from his father and squanders it on luxurious living. He reaches a point where he truly realizes that what he has done was wrong and seeks to make amends for it. Notice what scripture says about this.

> When he *came to his senses*, he said, "How many of my father's hired men have food to spare, and here I am starving to death! I will set out and go back to my father and say to him: Father, *I have sinned against heaven and against you. I am no longer worthy to be called your son*; make me like one of your hired men." So he got up and went to his father … The son said to him, "Father, I have sinned against heaven and against you. I am no longer worthy to be called your son." (Luke 15:17–21; emphasis mine)

Another example of godly sorrow is what happened after Jesus foretold that Peter would deny Him three times before the cock crowed in the morning. Peter denied this vehemently, but it came true, and scripture says, "The Lord turned and looked straight at Peter. Then Peter remembered the word the Lord had spoken to him: 'Before the rooster crows today, you will disown me three times.' And he went outside and wept bitterly" (Luke 22:61–62). When we, like both the prodigal and Peter, recognize our sin, and are truly sorry, we repent (i.e., we do all in our power to turn away from our sin and make amends for what we have done).

---

[11] J. W. MacGarvy, *Original Commentary on Acts*, Acts 2:41: "But another change had occurred within them. Under the influence of their new faith, they were pierced to the heart with a sense of guilt. This is the 'godly sorrow' which 'works repentance,' [2 Corinthians 7:10] and it prepared them to promptly obey Peter's command, 'Repent, and be immersed.' They repented, and were immersed."

This brings us to the next part of the statement, asking Jesus to be our Lord and Savior. The mere fact that we are sorry for our sins does not save us from the ultimate consequence of sin, which is eternal damnation. We must also realize that we can do nothing about our situation on our own. Only Jesus has the power of forgiveness, and we must ask for that forgiveness. "Therefore let it be known to you, brethren, that through Him forgiveness of sins is proclaimed to you" (Acts 13:38), and "repent of this wickedness of yours, and pray the Lord that if possible, the intention of your heart may be forgiven you" (Acts 8:22 NASB). Some people believe all we have to do to be right with God is pray the "Sinners Prayer"[12] to receive eternal salvation, but the Bible never says that. Rather, it says we must be obedient to Jesus. "He who believes in the Son has eternal life; but he who does not obey the Son shall not see life, but the wrath of God abides on him" (John 3:36). This is part of what it means to ask Jesus to be both our savior and master. We are saying to Him that we will follow His teachings and obey what He says. In asking for forgiveness, we are agreeing to obey and to serve Him.

---

[12] The Sinners Prayer has multiple versions. Some claim its origin as early as the sixteenth century in reaction to the Catholic Church dogma of justification. Others claim it had its origins in the eighteenth century revival movement. However, there is no documentary evidence to support either of these dates. Paul Chitwood of the Southern Baptist Theological Seminary states, "In addition to the Sinner's Prayer not occurring in the Bible, it is also absent from the pages of church history. We fail to see it even through the rise of revivalism and mass evangelism of the eighteenth and nineteenth centuries. In fact, research suggests that leading lost persons in praying the Sinner's Prayer is a relatively new method in evangelism. My studies have revealed no occurrence of the Sinner's Prayer before the twentieth century." In his research, Chitwood claims the earliest documentary evidence comes from use in the Billy Graham crusades (re: evangelistic tract *Steps to Peace with God*). Early in the 1950s, Bill Bright's Campus Crusade for Christ organization used the prayer in its teaching and training. Today the Sinners Prayer has become commonplace among televangelists and is found in numerous tracts throughout the world and in hundreds of languages.

The third part of the statement is the obedience part. This is where the "rubber meets the road!" Here we put into action the commitment we made to obey Jesus; this starts with baptism. This is the most controversial part of the statement; the church, in general, has modified the very form and function of baptism to the point where the writers of the New Testament would not recognize it. Without going into all the different doctrines regarding baptism, and without trying to debunk false teaching, let us look at the simplicity of baptism as stated in the scriptures. First, the Greek word used throughout the New Testament that gets translated baptism is BAPTIZO. At the time of the writing of the New Testament, the word meant to immerse something. If you are a coffee drinker and doughnut eater, you have probably baptized your doughnut at one time or another; you dunked it in the coffee. This is the simple meaning of the Greek word BAPTIZO.[13] This is the New Testament form of baptism.

The function of baptism is to demonstrate your obedience to the teaching of Jesus. Jesus Himself was baptized:

> Then Jesus came from Galilee to the Jordan to be baptized by John. But John tried to deter him, saying, "I need to be baptized by you, and do you come to me?" Jesus replied, "Let it be so now; it is proper for us to do this to fulfill all righteousness." Then John consented. As soon as Jesus was baptized, he went up out of the water. At that moment heaven was opened, and he saw the Spirit of God descending like a dove and lighting on him. And a voice from

---

[13] *Vine's Expository Dictionary of New Testament Words*: "to baptize," primarily a frequentative form of bapto, "to dip," was used among the Greeks to signify the dyeing of a garment, or the drawing of water by dipping a vessel into another, etc. Plutarchus uses it of the drawing of wine by dipping the cup into the bowl (Alexis, 67) and Plato, metaphorically, of being overwhelmed with questions (Euthydemus, 277 D).

heaven said, "This is my Son, whom I love; with him I am well pleased." (Matt. 3:13–17)

On the day that Peter preached to the crowd in Jerusalem, those who believed were baptized:

> Peter replied, "Repent and be baptized, every one of you, in the name of Jesus Christ for the forgiveness of your sins. And you will receive the gift of the Holy Spirit. The promise is for you and your children and for all who are far off—for all whom the Lord our God will call." With many other words he warned them, and he pleaded with them, "Save yourselves from this corrupt generation." Those who accepted his message were baptized, and about three thousand were added to their number that day. (Acts 2:38–41)

Later we read that the apostle Paul was also baptized: "Immediately, something like scales fell from Saul's[14] eyes, and he could see again. He got up and was baptized" (Acts 9:18). Jesus, on the day he ascended into heaven, following his resurrection, instructed the disciples to "make disciples of all nations, *baptizing them* in the name of the Father, and of the Son, and of the Holy Spirit" (Matt. 28:19; emphasis mine).

In Paul's letter to the church in Rome, he reiterates the form of baptism being by immersion and explains why we are to use this form.

> What shall we say, then? Shall we go on sinning so that grace may increase? By no means! We died to sin; how can we live in it any longer? Or don't you know that all of us who were baptized into Christ Jesus were baptized into his death? We were

---

[14] At the time, the apostle was known as Saul.

therefore buried with him through baptism into death in order that, just as Christ was raised from the dead through the glory of the Father, we too may live a new life. (Rom. 6:1–4)

For the Christian, baptism is being buried in the water just as Christ was buried in the tomb. We rise up from our watery grave just as Christ was raised from the tomb. The symbolism is unmistakable! Through baptism, we identify with Christ and His death and resurrection.

Baptism is an act of obedience that can only take place after a person acknowledges his or her sins, repents, and then acknowledges Jesus to be the Christ, the Son of God. The result of this act is that the person's sins are forgiven and he or she receives the gift of the Holy Spirit. "And Peter [said] to them, 'Repent, and let each of you be baptized in the name of Jesus Christ for the forgiveness of your sins; and you shall receive the gift of the Holy Spirit'" (Acts 2:38). Now, because of Jesus, one can say he or she has received life or eternal salvation. While men have conceived of a number of shortcuts to salvation, the fact is that this process, taught in the Bible, is the only way to receive eternal life!

HE LIVES WITHIN US

Another thing the Christian can expect from the Holy Spirit is that He will be living within the believer. We find back in the Old Testament that God promised the people of Israel that He would put His Spirit in them: "And I will put my Spirit in you and move you to follow my decrees and be careful to keep my laws" (Ezekiel 36:27). In the New Testament, we find similar statements; Jesus said, "And I will ask the Father, and he will give you another Counselor to be with you forever—the Spirit of truth. The world cannot accept him, because it neither sees him nor knows him. But you know him, for he lives with you and will be in you" (John 14:16–17). The apostle

Paul reminded the people in the church at Corinth of this saying, "Do you not know that your body is a temple of the Holy Spirit, who is in you, whom you have received from God? You are not your own" (1 Cor. 6:19).

Now take a deep breath because we are going to delve into some deep theology/psychology.[15] This has to do with the theology of humanity. How has the religious world viewed the origin of man, and how does that differ from how the nonreligious world has viewed man? From both a theological and a psychological perspective, humanity is viewed as consisting of both material and immaterial parts. The material parts are the flesh and bone parts. The flesh and bone give us form and structure. These are the parts we can see and touch. The immaterial parts are the life or soul of man. They are the parts that provide the "rationality, sensibility, intelligence, and freedom of will."[16] The separation of these two parts has been generally accepted throughout history. Jesus Himself acknowledged that humanity consisted of both body and soul. "Do not be afraid of those who kill the body but cannot kill the soul. Rather, be afraid of the One who can destroy both soul and body in hell" (Matt. 10:28). "Love the Lord your God with all your heart and with all your soul and with all your mind and with all your strength" (Mark 12:30). The apostle Paul also acknowledged the complexity of human nature. In his prayer for the church at Thessalonica, he wrote, "May God himself, the God of peace, sanctify you through and through. May your whole spirit, soul and body be kept blameless at the coming of our Lord Jesus Christ" (1 Thess. 5:23).

We need not make too much out of the fact that Paul separates soul and spirit, but since it does affect our discussion, we'll touch on it briefly. Scripture teaches four basic principles:

---

[15] Webster defines theology as "the study of religious faith, practice, and experience: the study of God and God's relation to the world." This differs from psychology, which is defined as the science or study of the mind and behavior: the way a person or group thinks.

[16] Tertullian, *Treatise on the Soul*, 38: http://mb-soft.com/believe/txv/tertullc.htm.

1. The soul and spirit are connected, but they are separable: "For the word of God is living and active. Sharper than any double-edged sword, it penetrates even to dividing soul and spirit, joints and marrow; it judges the thoughts and attitudes of the heart" (Hebrews 4:12).

2. The spirit of man connects us with God: "For who among men knows the thoughts of a man except the man's spirit within him" (1 Cor. 2:11). "God is spirit, and his worshipers must worship in spirit and in truth" (John 4:24).

3. Until we receive Christ as our Savior, we remain spiritually dead: "As for you, you were dead in your transgressions and sins, in which you used to live when you followed the ways of this world and of the ruler of the kingdom of the air, the spirit who is now at work in those who are disobedient. All of us also lived among them at one time, gratifying the cravings of our sinful nature and following its desires and thoughts. Like the rest, we were by nature objects of wrath. But because of his great love for us, God, who is rich in mercy, made us alive with Christ even when we were dead in transgressions—it is by grace you have been saved" (Eph. 2:1–5).

4. The spirit transforms the progression of life for the believer: "For this reason, since the day we heard about you, we have not stopped praying for you and asking God to fill you with the knowledge of his will through all spiritual wisdom and understanding. And we pray this in order that you may live a life worthy of the Lord and may please him in every way: bearing fruit in every good work, growing in the knowledge of God" (Col. 1:9–10).

Following the apostolic period, the church continued its belief in human dignity and the complexity of human nature. Much discussion centered on the immortality of the soul. Plato[17] had argued that the soul is eternal (i.e., it has neither beginning nor end). The early church disagreed with this, citing Adam's creation as the beginning of the human soul: "We have already decided one point in our controversy with Hermogenes, as we said at the beginning of this treatise, when we claimed the soul to be formed by the breathing of God, and not

---

[17] Plato (424/423 BC [a] – 348/347 BC).

out of matter. We relied even there on the clear direction of the inspired statement which informs us how 'the Lord God breathed on man's face the breath of life, so that man became a living soul.'"[18] Clement of Alexandria contended that while the human soul had its beginning in Adam, it would exist forever in the future, because of God's design: "It appears that the soul is not naturally immortal, but is made immortal by the grace of God, through faith and righteousness, and by knowledge."[19] Tertullian also argued that the soul was not only immortal, but the nature of the soul included "rationality, sensibility, intelligence, and freedom of the will."[20]

One of the basic questions that plagued the early church was whether soul and spirit are one and the same. While most agreed that they were, to varying degrees, others disagreed. Irenaeus, for example, claimed that man was created of body and soul. Upon conversion, the spirit was then added. Without the spirit, man was imperfect; however, man was meant to have a union of his soul with the spirit of God.[21] For our purpose, however, we need only to acknowledge that a part of human nature—soul or spirit is immortal. Recognizing this fact, we can understand how God can place His Spirit into the mortal part of our nature and connect with the immortal part.

HE BEARS FRUIT

The third thing we can expect from the indwelling of the Spirit is that we will begin to demonstrate a change of lifestyle. The biblical

---

[18] Tertullian, *Treatise on the Soul*, 3–4: http://mb-soft.com/believe/txv/tertullc.htm.

[19] Clement of Alexandria, *Fragment of Comments on 1 Peter.* 1:3: http://www.earlychristianwritings.com/text/clement-fragments.html.

[20] Tertullian, *Treatise on the Soul*, 38: http://mb-soft.com/believe/txv/tertullc.htm.

[21] Irenaeus, *Against Heresies*, 5.6.1 http://www.earlychristianwritings.com/text/irenaeus-book5.html.

term for this change process is *sanctification*. Sanctification is defined as (a) separated from evil to God: "who have been chosen according to the foreknowledge of God the Father, through the sanctifying work of the Spirit, for obedience to Jesus Christ and sprinkling by his blood" (1 Peter 1:2) and (b) a lifestyle befitting a follower of Christ: "I put this in human terms because you are weak in your natural selves. Just as you used to offer the parts of your body in slavery to impurity and to ever-increasing wickedness, so now offer them in slavery to righteousness leading to holiness. When you were slaves to sin, you were free from the control of righteousness. What benefit did you reap at that time from the things you are now ashamed of? Those things result in death! But now that you have been set free from sin and have become slaves to God, the benefit you reap leads to holiness, and the result is eternal life" (Rom. 6:19–22). Sanctification is God's will for every believer: "It is God's will that you should be sanctified: that you should avoid sexual immorality" (1 Thess. 4:3). So how does this sanctification take place? How can we go from following the ways of the world to following the ways of God? As unbelievers, we were addicted to sin, but as believers, we are expected to repent or turn away from sin, that we might become addicted to God: "My dear children, I write this to you so that you will not sin. But if anybody does sin, we have one who speaks to the Father in our defense—Jesus Christ, the Righteous One" (1 John 2:1).

Everyone has addictions. Some are good while others are bad. Every morning while eating breakfast I watch the morning news. I'm addicted to it! I could choose not to watch it, but I find a compelling desire to "check out what is going on in the world." While this may not be the best thing for me, because my stress level always seems higher after breakfast, I don't know that it is sinful. I have a friend who reads the Bible every morning when he gets up. That's a good addiction. He could choose not to do that, but he doesn't want to change. Scripture teaches that unbelievers are addicted to sin. They habitually choose to do things that are harmful and discredit God. Unfortunately, many Christians harbor sinful addictions as well, and while they struggle with their addictions, they often find that

Satan is still a dominant force in their lives, and the Holy Spirit is relegated to a backseat.

Addiction of any kind is hard to break. Smokers chew gum, stick on nicotine patches, exercise, and do anything else they can think of to try to quit smoking, but only a few find total relief. While my wife and I were serving as high school youth group leaders, I learned a lesson about quitting smoking. At the time, I smoked a pipe.

One day while taking the youth group on a weekend retreat in the north Georgia mountains, we pulled into a service station. This was back in the day when they were actually *service* stations. The owner came out to the bus I was driving and asked what he could do. I said, "Fill 'er up." I then walked over to the side of the road and calmly filled, packed, and lit my pipe as I enjoyed the brief break from driving.

After a few minutes of peaceful bliss, my thoughts were interrupted by one of our group's young ladies and her girlfriend. In all seriousness, they asked, "Mr. Shea, is it okay if we smoke too?" "No," I retorted, "and I shouldn't be smoking either!" I immediately put out my pipe and have not smoked since.

Now, you need to understand the attachment I had to my pipe. This may be something that only a pipe smoker can really understand. My pipe was my crutch. When asked a question, I would pack and poke and carefully light my pipe as I contemplated how I would answer. When under the stress of the moment, I would pack and poke and carefully light my pipe as my mind drifted off to more pleasant places. There were few things in this world that gave me more pleasure than my pipe! But in a flash that was all gone. The Holy Spirit moved, and I responded. For some time, I kept my pipe and a tin of tobacco, just in case, only to throw them out later without any sorrow whatsoever.

All this is to say that addictions are difficult to overcome, but "with God all things are possible" (Matt. 19:26). While scripture teaches that all things are possible with God, it also teaches that the Holy Spirit is the change agent for sanctification: "I have written you quite boldly on some points, as if to remind you of them again, because of the grace God gave me to be a minister of Christ Jesus to the Gentiles with the priestly duty of proclaiming the gospel of God, so that the Gentiles might become an offering acceptable to God, sanctified by the Holy Spirit" (Rom. 15:16). The Holy Spirit is the seed, which, when planted in us, brings forth a tree of new fruit. Paul said it this way: "But the fruit of the Spirit is love, joy, peace, patience, kindness, goodness, faithfulness, gentleness and self-control. Against such things there is no law" (Gal. 5:22). [22]

Much of the American population has lost its moral compass. An ever-growing percentage of persons have given in to things that were, until a few years ago, considered immoral and sinful. These things include the acceptance of the gay, lesbian, transgender community as perfectly normal. They also accept killing of one's child as a matter of choice. Pornography on television and in the movies has become a matter of progressive, and accepted, change in society. They consider all religions on an equal par with Christianity. They believe that lying, vulgarity, and hate are a normality, rather than sinfulness.

How did this change take place? I vaguely remember a book titled *The Frog in the Kettle*[23]. The theme of the book was illustrated by a frog and a kettle. If you place a live frog in a kettle of hot water, it will immediately jump out. Frogs don't like hot water. However, if you place a frog in a kettle of cold water and then slowly turn up the heat, the frog will sit in the water until it boils to death. The frog will adjust as the temperature goes up.

The church adjusts to culture in the same way. If culture makes an abrupt change, the church will react. However, if culture changes slowly, as it has with gay rights, abortion, and immorality in general, the church simply accepts these changes and often claims that biblical mandates against such things were, themselves, cultural issues and therefore not inspired teaching.

Politics, social policy, or laws cannot change these things. These things are matters of the heart, and we must change our hearts before we can get our moral compass back. This is what sanctification is

---

[22] See chapter 7.
[23] George Barna, Baker Publishing, 1990.

all about—a change of heart that comes about when the Holy Spirit comes to live within us. All the hate, anger, aggressive behavior, vulgarity, and hostility begin to melt away as the fruit of the Spirit begins to sprout in our lives.

We will look in more detail at the specific fruits of the Spirit in chapter 7.

HE SEALS THE CHRISTIAN

Recently I was reminded of how important one's signet ring was, especially back in the days prior to the nineteenth century. Kings, lords, and other important people used their rings, along with wax or other substances, to seal letters and other documents to prevent tampering. Upon the death of Christ, there was a concern among the chief priests and Pharisees that his disciples might come and steal the body. So they asked Pilate to secure the tomb. "'Take a guard,' Pilate answered. 'Go, make the tomb as secure as you know how.' So they went and made the tomb secure by putting a seal on the stone and posted a guard" (Matt. 27:65–66).

As Christians, God has sealed us with His Holy Spirit. Paul actually uses two analogies to show how God secures us in Christ: "And you also were included in Christ when you heard the message of truth, the gospel of your salvation. When you believed, you were marked in him with a seal, the promised Holy Spirit, who is a deposit guaranteeing our inheritance until the redemption of those who are God's possession—to the praise of his glory" (Eph. 1:13–14). First, by using the Holy Spirit as the sealing, and then second as a deposit, guaranteeing our eternal redemption. Most of us have had to make a deposit on something to ensure its availability when we were ready for it: rental cars are a good example. So God has placed a deposit on our lives to make sure when the time for the final redemption comes, we will be ready.

One of the questions that has plagued man since the beginning of the church is whether we can ever lose our salvation. Before we look at this issue, we need to understand that belief or disbelief in eternal security is not a matter of salvation. There is no litmus test that says if you disagree, you are not a true believer. I do believe, however, that it can influence your personal walk with Christ. Having stated this caveat, let us look at the teaching.

A number of prominent Christians teach, "Once saved, always saved." This is the doctrine of "eternal security" and the idea that once a person has accepted Christ, there is no possibility of ever losing that salvation. Teachers of eternal security use verses such as John 3:16: "For God so loved the world that he gave his one and only Son that whosoever believes in him should not perish, but have eternal life." The teaching then asks, "If God has given us something that can be lost, is it really eternal"?

Jack Wellman answers the question this way: "John 6:37 and John 10:28–29 both testify that once God calls you and saves you, He will not ever cast you away nor can you ever be snatched from Jesus' hand or the Father's hand. Philippians 1:6 says, 'being confident of this, that he who began a good work in you will carry it on to completion until the day of Christ Jesus.' Further, 1 Cor. 1:8 states, 'He will keep you strong to the end, so that you will be blameless on the day of our Lord Jesus Christ.' God does not call the qualified, but He qualifies the called. Holiness is not the way to Jesus; Jesus is the way to holiness. Your faithfulness is not based on your ability; it is your response to His ability."[24]

Unfortunately, few teachers of eternal security deal with those scriptures that argue against this teaching. Hebrews 6:1–6 is a good passage to study since it not only teaches that one can lose his or her salvation, but it is also one of the few passages that eternal security teachers attempt to discredit.

> Therefore let us leave the elementary teachings
> about Christ and go on to maturity, not laying again
> the foundation of repentance from acts that lead

---

[24] Jack Welman, http://www.whatchristianswanttoknow.com/can-a-christian-lose-their-salvation-a-biblical-analysis/#ixzz3m23YKaCZ.

to death, and of faith in God, instruction about baptisms, the laying on of hands, the resurrection of the dead, and eternal judgment. And God permitting, we will do so. It is impossible for those who have once been enlightened, who have tasted the heavenly gift, who have shared in the Holy Spirit, who have tasted the goodness of the word of God and the powers of the coming age, if they fall away, to be brought back to repentance, because to their loss they are crucifying the Son of God all over again and subjecting him to public disgrace."

There are four specific qualifiers here describing the individuals the author is referring to:

1. Who have once been enlightened.

    a. The Greek word here is *photizo*; meaning to give light to, light, shine on; bring to light, reveal, make known; enlighten, illumine (inwardly). So, to be enlightened about something is to come to an understanding of the topic.

    b. The opposition says that the person enlightened simply has a rudimentary knowledge about salvation, not an understanding that truly brings about repentance. However, if this is the case, why does the writer say, "it is impossible ... to be *brought back to repentance*," (emphasis mine) if the subject had never repented in the first place?

2. Have tasted of the heavenly gift.

    a. Presumably, the heavenly gift spoken of is salvation. It would be a stretch to think the author was writing of any other gift.

b. The opposition explains this as just getting the gift on the tip of the tongue, but not getting a full taste of the gift. This would be like receiving a piece of pie and taking one's fork, cutting off the very tip of the pie and tasting just a bit of that tip; never having gotten a complete taste.

3. Shared in the Holy Spirit.

a. To share in the Holy Spirit, as we read earlier, requires belief, repentance, and baptism. A nonbeliever does not have the Holy Spirit, nor does a person who may come to church and have heard of salvation but has never accepted Christ nor was baptized.

b. Some eternal security teachers claim that if one attends worship regularly but does not make a profession of faith, nor is that person baptized, they have shared in the Spirit vicariously.

4. Have tasted the goodness of the Word of God.

a. One can only see the Bible as goodness after he or she has been enlightened and recognized his or her sin and desires salvation. The precepts of the Old Testament condemn us, and the good news of the New Testament brings the goodness of the Word.

b. This takes on the same explanation as having tasted of the heavenly gift.

Numerous other passages state that one must stand firm to the end to be saved; verses such as Matthew 10:22: "You will be hated by everyone because of me, but the one who stands firm to the end will be saved"; Matthew 24:12: "Because lawlessness is increased, most people's love will grow cold. But the one who endures to the end, he will be saved"; and Luke 21:19: "But the one who endures to the end, he will be saved." Jesus is speaking in each of these verses. Why would He stress faithfulness to the end if salvation was guaranteed regardless of the heart and actions of man?

Tied directly to this are faith and works, or faith and obedience. Of what value is our faith if we fail to be obedient to Christ? To say, "remain faithful to the end" is the same as saying "remain obedient to the end." Take note of how James says this:

> What use is it, my brethren, if a man says he has faith, but he has no works? Can that faith save him? If a brother or sister is without clothing and in need of daily food, and one of you says to them, "Go in peace, be warmed and be filled," and yet you do not give them what is necessary for [their] body, what use is that? Even so faith, if it has no works, is dead, [being] by itself. But someone may [well] say, "You have faith, and I have works; show me your faith without the works, and I will show you my faith by my works." (James 2:14–18)

So the point is that Christ expects us, as His disciples, to be obedient to His teachings. We may fail in that along the way, but that will not cause us to lose our salvation; however, it might cause us to get so involved in the evils of this world that we deny Him and want nothing more to do with Him. If we were to reach that point, we may no longer want His salvation and would, of our own freewill, deny Him and the Spirit. In which case, it is impossible to be brought back to repentance. "For in the case of those who have once been enlightened and have tasted of the heavenly gift and have been made partakers of the Holy Spirit, and have tasted the good word of God and the powers of the age to come, and [then] have fallen away, it is impossible to renew them again to repentance, since they again crucify to themselves the Son of God, and put Him to open shame" (Heb. 6:4–6). To speak out against the Holy Spirit would be blasphemy of the Holy Spirit (Matt. 12:31–32; Luke 12:10).[25]

HE INTERPRETS THE CHRISTIANS' PRAYERS

Let's move on now to the next thing a believer might expect the Holy Spirit to do for him or her; that is that the Holy Spirit helps a believer to pray. We all need help when it comes to prayer. Even the disciples asked Jesus, "Lord, teach us to pray" (Luke 11:1). Jesus gave them what we refer to as the "Lord's Prayer" (Matt. 6:9–13). Today, both the Bible and the Holy Spirit teach us to pray. The problem is that for most of us, we pray from the heart, and the heart is fickle. Personal wants, opinions, concerns, and emotions cloud the pathway to God. Every true believer wants to pray the will of God, but there is often confusion just what God's will is. This may be where we need help.

Some believe this help comes in the form of a special private prayer language that only the Spirit and the Father understand. This belief comes primarily from Paul's comments to the church in Rome: "And in the same way the Spirit also helps our weakness; for we do not know how to pray as we should, but the Spirit Himself intercedes for [us] with groanings too deep for words; and He who searches the hearts knows what the mind of the Spirit is, because He intercedes for the saints according to the will of God" (Rom. 8:26–27).

Paul, however, is very explicit here. He clearly claims that this is a communication between the Holy Spirit (on behalf of the believer) and God. It is not in words, "too deep for words," but with, for lack of a better term, "groans." This is clearly not the same issue as tongues in the Corinthian letter, but it should not be glossed over lightly. Since prayer is our means of communication with God, it is important that we are clear about what we ask for. The problem lies in the complexity of our minds and hearts. We might know what we would like to have happen but are not sure if that is the right thing. It might also be the case where we know the right thing, but

---

[25] Blasphemy of the Holy Spirit is discussed in more detail on page 98.

in our hearts, we just can't seem to come to grips with it. Somehow, between our tears and cries out to God, the Holy Spirit intercedes and assures us that God understands and will do what is best.

In Paul's letter to the church at Corinth, he deals with the issue of speaking in tongues. Without going into all the theological issues, let's consider how the vast number of theologians explain the topic. In 1 Corinthians, chapter 14, Paul argues for orderly worship. He explains that speaking in tongues (an actual language unknown to the speaker) is of no benefit to the hearers unless someone is available to interpret. This is clearly the case of the apostles at Pentecost (Acts 2:1–4), where the apostles were speaking in languages unknown to them, but clearly understood by various ones of the hearers. However, at Corinth, it appears that people were speaking, but no one understood what was being said. There was no one who could interpret the language. The differences between this and the "groans" of the Holy Spirit in Romans 8 are: (1) here the speaker is the believer and in Romans 8 the speaker is the Holy Spirit, (2) here the speaking is audible and in Romans 8 it is silent, and (3) here it is interpretable and in Romans 8 it is not.

Never having prayed in a private prayer language, what I can say is that what Paul says can be applied to every believer. I could not begin to count the times I've found myself in a situation where my heart was breaking for someone who was undergoing severe tribulations. I knew what I wanted to see happen, but at the same time I questioned if that was the right thing for the person's own good. During prayer, my mind would race back and forth between what I wanted and what I thought was best. I'm sure the Holy Spirit spoke to God on my behalf because only God could understand what I was asking for.

This is not a matter of not knowing how to pray in general but how to pray in a specific situation. Scripture provides us with general principles that describe God's will. Using these principles, we can apply them to specific situations. In any case, I ask, knowing that God hears my prayers and will answer them (1 John 5:14–15). God knows what's best in each and every situation and knowing that gives me peace of mind.

HE GUIDES THE CHRISTIAN

Finally, we can expect the Spirit to be our guide: "For all who are being led by the Spirit of God, these are the sons of God" (Rom. 8:14). For such a short statement, this sure packs a wallop! The Spirit's guidance can be applied a number of different ways; it might be in how we respond to people, it might be in our own future actions, or it might be in what we are currently doing.

As I write this, the pope of the Catholic Church is visiting the United States. In several of his speeches, he has commented on the need to care for the poor, to combat evil, and to care for our environment. What I have not heard, however, is the need to combat our own passions, lusts, greed, and deceit.

This raises the question, Why do we need to be led by the Holy Spirit? Some of us remember the cartoon strip of Charlie Brown walking off the pitcher's mound mumbling, "Good grief! One hundred and eighty-four to nothing! I don't understand it … How can we lose when we're so sincere?!" I believe that is the way many Christians feel when life isn't going like they expected. So what's the problem? The problem is we live in a hostile environment controlled by Satan.

There is a lot of evil in the world. In fact, in the New Testament the word *world* is synonymous with evil. It is the kingdom of Satan: "Again, the devil took him to a very high mountain and showed him all the kingdoms of the world and their splendor. 'All this I will give you,' he said, 'if you will bow down and worship me'" (Matt. 4:8). The apostle John said, "All that is in the world, the lust of the flesh and the lust of the eyes and the boastful pride of life, is not from the Father, but is from the world" (1 John 2:16). James tells us the world, as Satan's domain, is the enemy of God: "You adulterous people, don't you know that friendship with the world is hatred toward God? Anyone who chooses to be a friend of the world becomes an enemy of God" (James 4:4).

The influence of the world affects every Christian far more than we would like to believe. We are dictated to by the government concerning our social and moral values, and the workplace affects how we interact with other people. If those relationships are positive, that can be a good thing, but when they go against the will and purpose of God, that's bad and it affects who and what we are. The apostle Paul said it best to the church in Corinth when he wrote, "Associating with bad people will ruin decent people" (1 Cor. 15:33 GW).

An example of what Paul was saying can be seen in today's church. In recent decades the church has become receptive to things that the church has condemned since the first century—things such as gay and lesbian lifestyles, abortion, and adultery. Rather than follow the lead of the Holy Spirit to righteousness, holiness, and Christ-centeredness, many a congregation has let the unholy spirit guide them down a path of acceptance of wickedness, inappropriate sexual acts, and self-centeredness. These are the very things that make the world an enemy of God.

How can the Holy Spirit lead us? It starts on our knees. We can begin to affect our own circumstances when we recognize that we have no control over other people and their circumstances. A recent movie, *War Room*, depicted a married couple who were having trouble. While the husband was completely absorbed in work, the gym, and other people, the wife was absorbed in her work and constantly complaining about her husband. Neither of them was paying any attention to their young daughter. God brought an older woman in contact with the wife. The older woman counseled her to let the Lord fight her battles for her instead of her fighting with her husband and losing all the time. To make a long story short, the wife learned to pray and to let the Holy Spirit lead her. This changed not only her life but the life of her husband and daughter as well.

Many people have lost the ability to pray, and without prayer, the Spirit cannot lead us. My father was an alcoholic. I remember, as a young child, my grandmother getting up at 2:00 a.m. daily to pray for my dad. By the time I was fifteen, my dad had quit drinking. I am convinced that the Holy Spirit led my dad to sobriety because of the prayers of my grandmother.

At the same time, one must be in the Word of God. We cannot expect the Holy Spirit to lead us when we have no idea where we're going. Only through constant study of the scriptures can we expect to learn about Jesus and the church. Only by studying the teaching of the apostles can we learn what kind of lives God expects from us and for us. Then, and only then, will we be able to look to the Holy Spirit for guidance, for the Holy Spirit speaks to us primarily through God's Word!

Do you want to live a more fruitful life? Do you want the confidence of having a Spirit-led life? Start today by asking the Lord, and let Him fill your life with love, happiness, and holiness. Don't quit when you get tired. Don't quit if you don't see results immediately. Remember our time is not the same as God's time: "But do not forget this one thing, dear friends: With the Lord a day is like a thousand years, and a thousand years are like a day" (2 Peter 3:8). Satan will do everything he can to discourage you. Don't let him win! You have the power through Jesus Christ to defeat Satan. James tells us: "Resist the devil and he will flee from you" (James 4:7). Tell Satan that he has no power over you and that you belong to the Lord, and "in the name of Jesus, *go away!*"

CHAPTER 4

The "Gift" of the Spirit

Inconsequence of identification with Jesus Christ and forgiveness of sins, we receive the gift of the Spirit as the second one of the divine gifts. The second benefit of repentance and baptism given in Acts 2:38 is this gift. Once sin, which separates us from God, has been removed by forgiveness, fellowship with him becomes appropriate. This fellowship with God operates most particularly with the Spirit of God whom Christ promised to be with us and in us after he ascended (Jn. 14:16–18). Therefore, the gift of the Spirit is not particularly a gift from the Spirit, but the gift of the Spirit. More strictly the gift is the relationship with the Spirit. He is a gift from God.[26]

The "gift of the Spirit" is not the same as "spiritual gifts." The gift of the Spirit is the fact that we receive the indwelling of the Holy Spirit Himself. Spiritual gifts, on the other hand, are defined as "varied endowments graciously bestowed by the triune God upon individual Christians, but particularly intended to enhance the community, worship, and service of locally gathered Christians and thereby to enrich the whole Church."[27]

---

[26] Warren, *What the Bible Says about Salvation*, 235.
[27] Bromiley 1988, 602.

There is more than one word in the Greek for *gift*. The word that most often translates spiritual *gifts* is the Greek word *char'isma*, and we'll deal with that later. Right now we are most interested in two other Greek words, *dō'ron* and *dōrea'*. The first word, dō'ron, means *gift* and is used of a variety of gifts. It is used of humans' gifts to one another in Matthew 2:11 and in Revelation 11:10; and of sacrifices in Matthew 5:23–24, 8:4, 15:5, 23:18–19; Hebrews 5:1, 8:3–4, 9:9, 11:4; of gifts of money in the temple in Luke 21:1, 4; and of God's gifts to humans in Ephesians 2:8.[28] The second word, *dōrea*, seems to be more legal than dō'ron, and denotes formal endowments. In the New Testament it is always used of the gift of God or Christ to humankind. It is only found in John 4:10 in the Gospels. In Acts, the Holy Spirit is called the dō'ron of God in 2:38, 8:20, 10:45, 11:17; also in Hebrews 6:4. Paul uses it more generally for the gifts of God or of Christ in Romans 5:15, 17; 2 Corinthians 9:15; Ephesians 3:7, 4:7. In the New Testament it always implies the grace of God.

This may seem trivial, but it is the foundation of the Christian belief. New believers, on more than one occasion, after baptism, have asked me if they should feel something, because they did not feel any different than they did before the baptism. One young Chinese woman asked, "Are you sure the Holy Spirit is with me? I don't feel anything." If you are a believer and have been obedient to the commands of Christ and have been baptized, you have the Holy Spirit! This is a fact stressed by scripture. On Pentecost, Peter told the people, "Repent, and let each of you be baptized in the name of Jesus Christ for the forgiveness of your sins; and you shall receive the gift of the Holy Spirit" (Acts 2:38).

This is a promise of God. We do not have to ask for the Holy Spirit as some claim. The promise is that the moment one is renewed, he or she receives the Holy Spirit. We do not have to beg God to give us a gift; He gives this freely, without strings attached. Notice what the apostle Paul wrote to the believers in Ephesus: "For by grace you have been saved through faith; and that not of yourselves, [it is]

---

[28] Kittle 1964, vol. 2, 166.

the gift of God; not as a result of works, that no one should boast" (Eph. 2:8–9).

Today a number of people rule out baptism as necessary for salvation and receiving the indwelling of the Holy Spirit. They cite passages of scripture that say believe and you shall receive eternal life (cf. John 3:16, 36; Rom. 10:8; and several others). So how does this idea harmonize with other statements that say baptism is necessary? The scriptures answer that question with the word *obedience*. Jesus's last command to His disciples was to "Go therefore and make disciples of all the nations, baptizing them in the name of the Father and the Son and the Holy Spirit, teaching them to observe all that I commanded you; and lo, I am with you always, even to the end of the age" (Matt. 28:19–20). How is a disciple made? Through baptism and obedience. In baptism one's sins are forgiven, and he or she receives the indwelling of the Holy Spirit (cf. Acts 2:38): "Those who *obey His commands* live in Him and He in them" (1 John 3:24; emphasis mine).

Until renewal, we are sinful people, lost in a sinful world. We struggle each day of our lives with the temptation to lie, cheat, steal, get involved in unacceptable sexual acts, and get caught up in addictions such as porn, alcohol, drugs, and any number of wicked and evil lifestyles. We find ourselves incapable of getting out of these situations on our own. While many people try solutions such as AA and self-help programs, these only deal with the symptoms of the sin, not the sin itself.

So what is the solution? The real solution is Jesus Christ! This is not to trivialize the difficulties faced by sinners but to acknowledge that we are incapable to combat sin on our own. When we accept the help that comes by acknowledging Jesus Christ as Lord and Savior, we receive the indwelling of the Holy Spirit, and only then do we have the power to combat sin and find peace in our lives.

Since so many Christians are unsure about their position with the Holy Spirit, it is only fair to discuss what happens when one receives the Spirit. We find in the New Testament three primary ways in which the Spirit came upon people: unsolicited (e.g., Pentecost), with the laying on of hands by an apostle, and, lastly, in baptism.

The first way, unsolicited, happened on Pentecost and at the household of Cornelius (Acts 10:17–48). Up to this time, only Jews had received the Holy Spirit. However, "While Peter was still speaking these words, the Holy Spirit fell upon all those who were listening to the message. And all the circumcised believers who had come with Peter were amazed, because the gift of the Holy Spirit had been poured out upon the Gentiles also" (Acts 10:44–45). This situation was unique since this was the first time Gentiles received the Word of God. To convince Peter and those Jews who were with him that God had given His Spirit to the Gentiles, He also gave them the gift of speaking in tongues.

The second way was by the laying on of hands by an apostle, which we find in Acts 8:17–19 and 9:12–18. The first case involved the Samaritans. Jews looked down on the Samaritans primarily because they were considered to be half-breeds who did not adhere to proper Jewish doctrine. Real Jews were not allowed to have any contact with Samaritans. When the apostles in Jerusalem heard the Samaritans had received the Word of God, they sent Peter and John to them. Even though these new believers had been baptized, they had not yet received the Holy Spirit. Peter and John began praying for them and laying hands on them, and they began receiving the Holy Spirit.

The second case involved Saul of Tarsus. He was a strict orthodox Jew who was persecuting the church. He was on his way to Damascus to round up the believers and take them back to Jerusalem to be punished. On the way, the Lord confronted him. After being struck blind by the Lord, Saul was taken on to Damascus and taken to the home of Judas, where he stayed for three days, blind and without food or drink.

In the meantime, a disciple named Ananias had a vision from the Lord telling him to go to Judas's home and talk to Saul. Ananias was reluctant to go because he had heard about Saul's reputation. Ananias went and entered the house, where he laid hands on Saul and said, "Brother Saul, the Lord Jesus, who appeared to you on the road by which you were coming, has sent me so that you may regain your sight, and be filled with the Holy Spirit." One can read the result of this in Acts 9:10–20.

The third way, which was the regular way, was through baptism. There is a story told in Acts 8:25–38 about the apostle Philip and the treasurer to Queen Candice, queen of the Ethiopians. The treasurer was returning home after being in Jerusalem. He was reading a scroll from the prophet Isaiah. Philip joined him and asked if he understood what he was reading. He responded no, and Philip "preached Jesus to him." After listening to Philip he believed and, as there was water nearby, asked what prevented him from being baptized. "And he gave orders to stop the chariot. Then both Philip and the eunuch went down into the water and Philip baptized him" (Acts 8:38).

No mention is made of the eunuch (treasurer) receiving the Holy Spirit. Other than a brief statement that he "went on his way rejoicing," he is not mentioned again in scripture. The point is that baptism is the normal way people received the Holy Spirit then and now. There are no miraculous tongues of fire, speaking in other languages, or other phenomenal activity that need to take place. It is simply the action of God, as promised by Christ, that those who believe will receive another Helper. While there are cases, mostly in third world countries where the Word of God is being proclaimed for the first time, where we hear of miraculous healings or people speaking in tongues, in association with baptism, documentation is often sketchy. Sometimes we have firsthand reports, but other times it comes down to, "I was told by _____," you fill in the blank. It must be said that this is not to be confused with miracles in general. Miracles take place every day, whether we are aware of them or not. The point is that such things need not take place for one's baptism to be complete.

There is another doctrine concerning the "Holy Spirit" and "baptism." This is referred to as "baptism of the Holy Spirit" or "baptism by fire." It is believed to follow water baptism and is attributed to John Wesley.[29] This doctrine teaches there is a second work of grace that "eradicates sinful desire entirely and leaves 'perfect love' to God and man as henceforth the only motive of the heart."[30]

This movement, known as the holiness movement, spawned a variety of beliefs that require the Holy Spirit to descend upon the believer in order that the believer might achieve a second work of grace, or sanctification.

Keswick holiness came out of the Keswick Convention in England in 1875. Differing from Wesleyan holiness, Keswick holiness does not claim to eradicate sin; rather, it is a Spirit-filling that assists the believer in the ongoing battle against the powers of evil. This results in a "faith-based" fight. It shifts the burden of the fight off the shoulders of the individual onto the shoulder of the Spirit. "Slogans like 'let go and let God', 'stop trying and start trusting', pinpoint this imperative."[31]

A short time later, Pentecostalism found its way onto the religious stage. Pentecostal holiness has its roots back "to 1 January 1901, when Miss Agnes Ozman, a student at Bethel Bible College, Topeka, Kansas, spoke in tongues after the principal, Charles Fox Parham (1873–1929), laid hands on her and prayed for her to receive the power of the Holy Spirit."[32] After this, Pentecostalism spread rapidly throughout the nation. In 1906, in Los Angeles, California, a revival, known as the Azusa Street Revival, was characterized by dramatic activities such as healings, speaking in tongues, and people being slain in the Spirit. The result of this event was that Pentecostalism spread throughout the nation and is continuing to grow throughout the rest of the world.

---

[29] John Wesley (1703–91) was the older brother of Charles Wesley, the hymn writer). "In 1729 he … became the spiritual leader of the small group of students his brother Charles had gathered. This band was called the 'Holy Club' by other students; later they were known as 'Methodists'" (Sinclair B 1988).

[30] Ferguson and Wright, *New Dictionary of Theology*, 318.

[31] Ibid., 314.

[32] Ibid., 503.

These two groups, often referred to as "holiness" groups, hold in common the idea that there is a second level of holiness that comes only to those who receive the "baptism of the Spirit" in addition to water baptism. This "baptism" comes about only through prayer, personal piety, and/or the laying on of hands. However, I find nothing in scripture to give credence to this theory. There are passages that refer to other baptisms, such as Luke 12:50: "'I came to cast fire on the earth, and would that it were already kindled! I have a baptism to be baptized with, and how great is my distress until it is accomplished!'" Here Jesus appears to be referencing His suffering and death.

The New Testament notes "one Lord, one faith, one baptism; one God and Father of all, who is over all and through all and in all" (Eph. 4:5). The apostle Paul said, "'John's baptism was a baptism of repentance. He told the people to believe in the one coming after him, that is, in Jesus.' On hearing this, they were baptized into the name of the Lord Jesus. When Paul placed his hands on them, the Holy Spirit came on them, and they spoke in tongues and prophesied" (Acts 19:4). The apostle Peter uses Noah's experience in the flood when referring to baptism: "God waited patiently in the days of Noah while the ark was being built. In it only a few people, eight in all, were saved through water, and this water symbolizes baptism that now saves you also—not the removal of dirt from the body but the pledge of a good conscience toward God" (1 Pet. 3:20–21). Each of these references only a single baptism, with water, not a second baptism by the Holy Spirit.

CHAPTER 5

Spiritual Gifts

We need to shift our attention from the gift *of* the Spirit to spiritual gifts. We said earlier there were several different Greek words for gift. The New Testament uses the word *dōrea'*, to refer to the gift of God or Christ to men (i.e., the Holy Spirit). *Vine's Expository Dictionary* defines the word *charisma* (*charisma*), however, as "His endowments upon believers by the operation of the Holy Spirit in the churches."[33] C. Peter Wagner uses this definition: "A spiritual gift is a special attribute given by the Holy Spirit to every member of the Body of Christ, according to God's grace, for use within the context of the Body."[34]

It is extremely important for any group of believers wishing to fulfill their purpose before God to know and understand both the purpose of these gifts and who in the body receives them. For the answer to these two questions, we again turn to scripture. The apostle Peter tells us, "As *each* has received a gift, employ it for one another, as good stewards of God's varied grace" (1 Pet. 4:10; emphasis mine). The apostle Paul, who wrote prolifically on spiritual gifts, reminds us, "It was he who gave some to be apostles, some

---

[33] Vine, *Vine's Expository Dictionary of the New Testament*, 487.
[34] Wagner, *Discover Your Spiritual Gifts*, 18.

to be prophets, some to be evangelists, and some to be pastors and teachers, to prepare God's people for works of service, *so that the body of Christ may be built up* until we all reach unity in the faith and in the knowledge of the Son of God and become mature, attaining to the whole measure of the fullness of Christ" (Eph. 4:11–13; emphasis mine). And "So with yourselves; since you are eager for manifestations of the Spirit, strive to excel *in building up the church*" (1 Cor. 14:12 RSV; emphasis mine).

Every born-again believer has one or more spiritual gifts that are to be used for the building up of the church. Unfortunately, many believers either do not believe this or do not know what their gift is. This should never be. Paul reminded the Corinthian Christians, "Now, concerning spiritual gifts, brethren, I do not want you to be ignorant" (1 Cor. 12:1). The topic of this book is the Holy Spirit, not spiritual gifts. Therefore, we will leave the details of the spiritual gifts up to others. Here we will only give an overview.

Several passages in the New Testament list spiritual gifts. None is all-inclusive. There are three primary lists as follows:

Romans 12:6–8 mentions the following gifts:

1. Prophesy: The Greek word means to preach an intelligible message of God, as opposed to speaking in tongues (1 Cor. 14:6, 22). This may or may not include the telling of future events.

2. Service: Ministering in all forms. It includes work both inside the church as well as outside.

3. Teaching: This does not have to be in a formal setting such as a Sunday school class. It may include small group Bible studies or one on one.

4. Exhortation: Console, comfort, cheer up, encourage, and stimulate another's faith. It too can be one on one or in a

formal setting. It may be the greeter at the door or just the smile of a person walking through the hallway.

5. Giving: This can be in the form of money, material objects, or assistance. This is the gift of generosity. It could be to the local church, a missionary, or to a homeless shelter in the name of God.

6. Leadership: The authority and ability to lead, manage, and organize, so that others are inspired to follow.

7. Mercy: Demonstrate care and concern for others. To sympathize with and comfort the sorrowing.

1 Corinthians 12:8–10, 28 adds these:

8. Wisdom: Insight into the true nature of things, especially in spiritual matters. According to Trench, "Augustine made this distinction between sophia and gnosis: 'These are usually distinguished so that wisdom [sophia] pertains to the understanding of eternal matters, but knowledge [gnosis] to those things which we experience through the senses of the body.'"[35]

9. Knowledge: This is more than a general knowledge. It is an esoteric or specialized knowledge: knowing things that only a few people may know.

10. Faith: "Now faith is being sure of what we hope for and certain of what we do not see" (Heb. 11:1). While each of us must have faith to accept Christ as Savior, some people have a faith that exceeds that. This has to do specifically with spiritual issues not human issues. This is not the same

---

[35] Trench, *Synonyms of the New Testament*, 281.

as believing something is going to happen simply because you want it to happen.

11. Healing: Used generally in the New Testament as the ability to cure physical ailments, although it can mean spiritual healing as well.

12. Miracles: The ability to perform works of supernatural origin that could not be produced by natural means. This is more than doing something extraordinary.

13. Discerning of spirits: Knowing the difference between good and evil in spiritual matters.

14. Tongues: This can be in one of two forms: speaking in a known language, which the speaker has never learned, or speaking in an ecstatic utterance, which requires some form of interpretation. The first is better than the second is, since it edifies the entire body of believers. Unless it is interpreted, the second edifies only the speaker. The apostle Paul wrote, "Tongues, then, are a sign, not for believers but for unbelievers; prophecy, however, is for believers, not for unbelievers" (1 Cor. 14:22).

15. Interpretation of tongues: The ability to interpret tongues, either a known language or ecstatic utterance.

16. Apostle: A person who is sent with a message. The twelve, plus Paul, were chosen by Jesus, specifically to carry His message to the world after He ascended.

17. Helps: This could be anything that could be done to assist people in need, such as the poor, homeless, disabled, etc.

18. Administration: The ability to administrate, organize, and direct people, projects, and/or programs just as Jesus intends.

Finally, Ephesians 4:11 adds:

19. Evangelist: To be a messenger of the good news of the gospel. Similar to a preacher but generally not responsible solely for a single body of believers.

20. Pastor: The ability to be responsible for spiritually caring for, protecting, guiding, and feeding a group of believers entrusted to one's care.

While classic Pentecostalism only accepts nine of these gifts:[36] wisdom, knowledge, faith, healing, miracles, prophesy, discerning of spirits, tongues, and interpretation of tongues, Wagner adds these five gifts:[37]

21. Celibacy (1 Cor. 7:7): To voluntarily remain single without regret and with the ability to maintain controlled sexual impulses so as to serve the Lord without distraction.

22. Voluntary poverty (1 Cor. 13:3): To purposely live an impoverished lifestyle to serve and aid others with your material resources

23. Martyrdom (1 Cor. 13:3): The ability to give over one's life to suffer or to be put to death for the cause of Christ.

24. Missionary (Eph. 3:6–8): The ability to carry out ministry in a culture other than one's own.

25. Hospitality (1 Pet. 4:9): The ability to warmly welcome people, even strangers, into one's home or church as a means of serving those in need of food or lodging.

---

[36] Wagner, *Discover Your Spiritual Gifts*, 39.
[37] Ibid., 27.

While most born-again believers would agree with the idea that the Holy Spirit helps guide their lives, many have no understanding how that happens. If we are, as the apostle Paul said, "Eager for manifestations of the Spirit, strive to excel in building up the church" (1 Cor. 14:12), then we must know what our individual gifts are and how we might employ them in building up the church.

In any given body of believers, God provides the gifts necessary to build up that body: to fulfill the purpose God has for that particular body. Have you ever noticed how different congregations have different strengths? Some churches have a strong music program that attracts members of the community. Other churches may have a strong youth program that reaches out to the youth of the community. Another church may have a strong small-groups ministry that emphasizes personal growth and evangelism. The church my wife and I attend has a strong preaching ministry coupled with music that reaches out and evangelizes college students. For any of these churches to grow, God endows the members of the church with all of the gifts necessary for them to fulfill their particular ministry. For this reason, the apostle Paul could say to the church in Corinth, "You are not lacking in any gift" (1 Cor. 1:7).

Believers at any stage of maturity may discover a new gift if the Holy Spirit determines the gift is needed and that individual is the one who should have it. While gifts may vary among individuals in any body of believers, there is something consistent that each and every believer should be demonstrating in his or her life, and that is the fruit of the Spirit.

—————— CHAPTER 6 ——————

Fruit of the Spirit

There is a major difference between spiritual gifts and the fruit of the Spirit. While the Holy Spirit gives one or more gifts to each Christian, we do not automatically receive the fruit of the Spirit. None of us receive all the gifts of the Spirit, but we are, each one, expected to develop each of the fruits listed in Galatians 5:22. They are part of each of us, which we express in our personalities to one degree or another. What the Holy Spirit does is work with each of these to enhance them and make them more dominate in our lives. Paul speaks of this change in our lives extensively in his letter to the church at Ephesus (Eph. 4:17–32). So let's look at each one briefly:

LOVE

This is the foundation of the Christian life. The apostle Paul taught that without love there would be no difference between the followers of Christ and the rest of the world. However, we need to understand that this love is different from the love the rest of the world strives for.

Love, depicted in the United States, by Hollywood, is an erotic, self-sensuous love. Love is used to express any emotional attachment, such as, "I love my car, "or "I love my dog." We can use it to mean different things in the same sentence, so "I love my wife, and I love her cooking." Hopefully, love, here, has two different meanings. So in English we find one word expressing an array of different emotions. However, four words in the Greek language get translated *love* in English. *Eros* is a sexual kind of love and the kind most often used by Hollywood. *Storge* is family love, the bond among mothers, fathers, sisters, and brothers. Neither eros nor storge are found in the Bible. In the New Testament, two words that get translated *love* are *philia* and *agape*. Philia is a close friendship or brotherly love. It is used twenty-five times in the New Testament. The word agape is used, both as a noun and a verb, a total of 221 times in the New Testament and is the word found listed in the fruit of the Spirit. It is an unconditional kind of love, not without emotion, but a love by choice. Agape is expressed when Jesus said, "For God so loved the world that he gave his one and only Son, that whoever believes in him shall not perish but have eternal life" (John 3:16). The apostle John tells of a time after the resurrection of Jesus when He appeared to six of His disciples who were out fishing. Jesus was on the shore and called out to them, "Haven't you any fish?"

"No," they responded.

Jesus told them to throw their nets over the other side of the boat. When they did, their nets filled with so many fish they couldn't haul them all up. At that, John recognized Jesus and said to Peter, "It's the Lord!" Peter immediately jumped into the water and swam to shore. When the others got to shore, they all ate breakfast together.

After breakfast, Jesus asked Peter, "Simon, son of John, do you truly love [agape] me more than these?"

Peter answered, "Yes, Lord, you know I love [philia] you."

Again, Jesus asked him, "Simon, son of John, do you truly love [agape] me?"

Peter answered, "Yes, Lord, you know I love [philia] you."

The third time Jesus said to him, "Simon, son of John, do you love [philia] me?"

John said that Peter was hurt because Jesus asked the third time, "Do you love [philia] me?"

Peter answered, "Lord, you know all things; you know that I love [philia] you."

Now the point here is to note that Jesus uses one term, agape, the first two times, but, philia, the third time. Peter uses philia, all three times. Philia is a conditional love that expects philia in return. Agape, on the other hand, is unconditional. It is given by choice, whether it receives agape in return or not.

JOY

Life today seems filled with nothing but evil. Crime is rampant. Terrorism is on the news every night. From automobile accidents to terminal illnesses, from financial woes to hunger, people seem plagued with nothing but bad news. It seems strange to see someone smiling today. However, for the Christian, life doesn't have to be that way. Joy is an attribute that each Christian can learn to display in his or her life. This comes about when we come to the realization that God is truly in control of all things. No matter what life throws at us, we can be confident that God knows what we are going through and has the ability to heal us in our pain, strengthen us in our weakness, and comfort us in sorrow. It is the same today as it has been throughout history. God is no less capable of changing the circumstances in each of our lives today as He did in the lives of Moses, David, and Esther in the Old Testament, and Peter, Paul, and Mary in the New Testament.

PEACE

We are living today in a world of high anxiety. Life is speeding by us so fast it seems impossible to keep up. We have no control over most of the changes and concerns that occupy our minds. The economy is extremely fragile today, and we are warned constantly by financial experts that the stock market may soon implode and wipe out our savings; more and more people are losing their jobs, either to overseas workers or to automation. The divorce rate continues to climb, and fewer and fewer people are getting married because of the potential for a broken family. More and more families are on welfare or government subsidies so they can have food to eat or health care. With all this happening, it is easy to lose any sense of peace or tranquility.

However, as Christians we don't have to be part of the group of people living in fear and with troubled hearts, because we know "the peace of God, which transcends all understanding, will guard your hearts and your minds in Christ Jesus" (Phil. 4:7). That peace is there, available to each of us who have the Holy Spirit. Without the peace of God operating in your life, you could become very easily rattled, shaken, and tormented, and your trust in God could falter the first time any kind of adversity should ever come your way. However, the peace of God wipes all the storm clouds away.

PATIENCE

This is another place where the fast pace of today's lifestyle wreaks havoc. Consider the road rage we hear about today. Maybe you've even expressed a little of that while driving. Or consider how short-tempered people can get while standing in line at the grocery store or at the gas pumps. Some even go to extremes because of a lack of patience and cause bodily harm to other people. I watched on the news one day as a driver of a car ran a bicyclist off the road because he had to wait to get around him.

For a number of Christians this can be a major problem. When we want something, we want it now—not next week, next month, or even tomorrow, but now. This may come across regularly in our prayer life. If I pray for something, I want to see the answer to that prayer now. However, God operates on a different time schedule than we do. He is not bound by a twenty-four-hour day or a seven-day week. He operates outside the realm of time. As Peter tells us, "With the Lord a day is like a thousand years, and a thousand years are like a day" (2 Pet. 3:8). God can afford to take His time; He has nothing but time. Another thing to consider is that God has perfect timing. Sometimes what we ask for is not ready yet; this is not the time for it, so we must wait.

After graduating from Bible college, my wife and I moved to Kansas City. I was optimistic about reclaiming the world for Christ. But I soon found my hopes dashed when after sending out almost a hundred copies of my resume, I did not receive one single response.

Since I also had a graduate degree in computer science, I decided to start a computer consulting business. To help pay the mortgage, etc., I accepted a consulting/programming job with Centerre Bank in Kansas City, developing a human resource information system. Night after night, I would ask God to find me a located ministry, often ending the prayer in tears. One day while returning from Fort Leavenworth, Kansas, I was complaining as usual to God because I couldn't find a place to preach. All of a sudden I heard a voice. The voice was so clear that I pulled over to the side of the road. The voice said, "When you learn to care for the flock I've given you, I'll give you another flock." Without a thought, I shouted back, "That's the problem, Lord. You haven't given me a flock!" Again the voice repeated, "When you learn to care for the flock I've given you, I'll give you another flock." Several minutes went by, and there was no sound.

I got back on the road and wondered if I really hear what I thought I had. After returning home, I told my wife about the voice. What could it mean?

The next day I was walking through the hall of the bank when the vice president for personnel called, "Bill, when you get a minute, I'd like to talk to you." Since she was in charge of the project, I turned around and went into her office. We had spent several minutes discussing the project when she suddenly changed the topic and began talking about the church and issues she was having at home. I offered my thoughts and comfort, we prayed together, and I continued on my way.

Later that night, a light came on! Was that my flock? Were the people God had already brought into my life the one's I was supposed to be ministering to? A businessman I know had once said successful businesspeople look to other successful businesspeople for guidance, not to the preacher. After that, I watched closely for opportunities to offer comfort and share the gospel of Jesus Christ.

A few months later, one of my daughters was looking to get married and asked me to perform the service. She had chosen the Crestview Christian Church in Manhattan, Kansas. At the time, Crestview did not have a regular preacher, so they asked if I'd like to stay over after the wedding on Saturday and preach on Sunday. I said, "Sure!" One of the elders mentioned they were accepting resumes and asked if I would be interested in sending them mine. A little over a month later, I was welcomed into the congregation as the new minister.

"When you learn to care for the flock I've given you, I'll give you another flock." Several months prior, the Holy Spirit had offered both comfort and counsel. Now here I was fulfilling my calling for God. It became obvious that I was not ready for Crestview, nor was Crestview ready for me, when I graduated and earnestly prayed for a located ministry. Nevertheless, God's time was perfect, and I spent thirteen years ministering to that flock of believers.

KINDNESS

Because of more people being impatient, having short fuses, and with everyone always being in a hurry, many people have lost the ability to treat others with kindness and respect. Just try getting into traffic on a busy street. Try getting out of a football stadium at the end of the game. People can get downright hostile when they are in a hurry and lose any sense of kindness that they might otherwise show. In politics, a difference of ideology can turn neighbors into enemies. Even something as simple as a tree that needs pruning but is sitting on the property line can bring about a lawsuit.

For the Christian, these things offer an opportunity to demonstrate the fruit of kindness in our lives. Abraham Lincoln once said, "The best way to defeat an enemy is to make him a friend." When we are friends, we can discuss our differences rationally, without hostility and animosity. Would you like to see a change in people? Try walking down a street and look people in the eye with a smile on your face and offer a simple greeting of "Hello." You will be amazed at how many people will smile and greet you back! Kindness goes hand in hand with the fruit of love. When you have the love of God flowing through you, you cannot help but demonstrate kindness as well.

GOODNESS

Goodness is a moral issue. It is the state of being good—the opposite of being bad. The moral compass of America began changing dramatically in the late sixties. Things that were once held dear began to fall as we moved into the age of self-realization. This was an age when emotions, not logic or tradition, governed our actions. Homosexuality soon became acceptable and in some places even fashionable. A woman's body belonged to her and the number of abortions rose dramatically. Men became a law unto themselves, and protests against the Vietnam War turned violent. Even a number of Christian denominations began to turn against the teachings of scripture and accepted the social arguments presented at the time. Since then things have only gotten worse, and the church is no longer a haven of righteousness and goodness, where the teachings of Christ are followed. Instead, people are invited into the church without any expectation of them changing their lifestyles. Even the pastors and teachers in many of those churches are living lifestyles in opposition to the teachings of Christ.

As believers grow in their faith and understanding, their morality should grow as well. The idea of goodness, or being good, should be something every Christian strives for. Goodness, holiness, and righteousness all fall into the same category, as Christians are called to goodness:

> And concerning you, my brethren, I myself also am convinced that you yourselves are full of goodness, filled with all knowledge, and able also to admonish one another. (Rom. 15:14)

> For you were formerly darkness, but now you are light in the Lord; walk as children of light (for the fruit of the light [consists] in all goodness and righteousness and truth), trying to learn what is pleasing to the Lord. And do not participate in the unfruitful deeds of darkness, but instead even expose them; for it is disgraceful even to speak of the things which are done by them in secret. (Eph. 5:8–12)

> Now for this very reason also, applying all diligence, in your faith supply moral excellence, and in [your] moral excellence, knowledge; and in [your] knowledge, self-control, and in [your] self-control, perseverance, and in [your] perseverance, godliness; and in [your] godliness, brotherly kindness, and in [your] brotherly kindness, love. (2 Pet. 1:5–7)

FAITHFULNESS

The scripture has much to say concerning faith and faithfulness. In the twenty-first century, faith has gotten a lot of bad press. It is often depicted as a simple-mindedness, belief in myths and old wives' tales, or the actions of the uneducated. Today, many see themselves as too sophisticated and intelligent to accept those tired old beliefs.

But faith is essential in our relationship to God, and faithfulness is the demonstration of that faith.

The author of Hebrews begins his passage on faith by saying, "Now faith is being sure of what we hope for and certain of what we do not see" (Heb. 11:1). He then stresses the importance of faith, saying, "Without faith it is impossible to please God, because anyone who comes to him must believe he exists and that he rewards those who earnestly seek him" (Heb. 11:6). The rest of the passage is a demonstration of both faith and faithfulness. We might define faithfulness as the demonstration of faith itself. One of the individuals referenced in Hebrews is Abraham. He is also one of the most referenced individuals of faithfulness in the Old Testament.[38] The story begins with God telling Abraham that he is to take his only son, Isaac, whom he loved, and offer him as a burnt offering. God had previously promised Abraham that his descendants would be as numerous as the sand on the seashore. So it made no sense to Abraham that he should now offer up his only son to die, but he trusted (i.e., had faith) that God would keep his promise. Therefore, Abraham took Isaac and went to the place God had directed. There he built an altar and placed Isaac upon it. Just as he was about to plunge the knife into Isaac's body, "the angel of the LORD called out to him from heaven, 'Abraham! Abraham!' 'Here I am,' he replied. 'Do not lay a hand on the boy,' he said. 'Do not do anything to him. Now I know that you fear God, because you have not withheld from me your son, your only son'" (Gen. 22:11–12). Then a ram appeared in the thicket close by. Abraham removed Isaac and offered up the ram instead. The point is that Abraham's belief that God would fulfill His promise resulted in the act of faithfulness on the part of Abraham.

Today, many people put their trust into things of this world. They put their faith in the things they love the most. The apostle Paul spoke to this in his letter to Timothy: "But mark this: There will be perilous times in the last days. People will be lovers of themselves, lovers of money, boastful, proud, abusive, disobedient to their

---

[38] See the testing of Abraham in Genesis 22.

parents, ungrateful, unholy, without love, unforgiving, slanderous, without self-control, brutal, not lovers of the good, treacherous, rash, conceited, lovers of pleasure rather than lovers of God—having a form of godliness but denying its power. Have nothing to do with them" (2 Tim. 3:1–5).

Our faithfulness depends completely on what we consider to be of great importance—things that we value. When money is of great importance, our actions will be to conserve it or hoard it. We come under great stress when we fear losing it. At the time of this writing, the stock market lost over 20 percent in a matter of a couple of weeks. This is a major topic of discussion wherever money is of great importance. Large numbers of people fear losing vast sums if it does not turn around. The result is frantic selling of stock before it drops more, and the result of all that selling is that stocks drop even further. We see this same thing in marriage. When a couple truly values their marriage, they do all they can to strength it and make it better. They avoid actions that will lessen the relationship and cause it to fail. When we fail to place importance on marriage, or devalue marriage by turning it into something God never meant it to be, the result is disastrous. Many a marriage has started out with a bright future. However, as time goes by, boredom in the marriage sets in. We see others who appear to be having a more robust and joyful marriage than we have. So simple flirtation or confiding in a member of the opposite sex soon leads to something more serious, and before we know it, we are talking about divorce. My wife and I are in a second marriage. But we agreed before we married that divorce would not be a word in our vocabulary and that by placing extreme importance on our marriage and committing ourselves and our marriage to God, we could work through anything. That was thirty-eight years ago. We have weathered a lot, but praise be to God it has only gotten better.

Our relationship with God has to take on an even greater importance. Jesus taught we had to be willing to give up everything for him: "Then Jesus said to his disciples, 'If anyone would come after me, he must deny himself and take up his cross and follow me'" (Matt. 16:24). To another he said, "If you want to be perfect, go, sell your possessions and give to the poor, and you will have treasure in heaven. Then come, follow me" (Matt. 19:21). Another time he said, "'Follow me.' But the man replied, 'Lord, first let me go and bury my father.' Jesus said to him, 'Let the dead bury their own dead, but you go and proclaim the kingdom of God.' Still another said, 'I will follow you, Lord; but first let me go back and say good-by to my family.' Jesus replied, 'No one who puts his hand to the plow and looks back is fit for service in the kingdom of God'" (Luke 9:59–62). Through the power of the Holy Spirit and the fruit he helps grow in our lives, we can have this kind of faithfulness in our own personal relationship with God. Faithfulness is not immediately mature when we accept Christ, but like fruit on the tree that is properly cultivated, fertilized, and pruned, it will grow stronger year by year.

GENTLENESS

The apostle Paul wrote to the church at Corinth: "Shall I come to you with a whip, or in love and with a gentle spirit?" (1 Cor. 4:21). Again, "By the meekness and gentleness of Christ, I appeal to you" (2 Cor. 10:1). In addition, to the church at Philippi, Paul wrote, "Let your gentleness be evident to all" (Phil. 4:5). Gentleness is a vitally important attribute in the Christian's life. The world is already full of evil, violence, and hostility. While we are to be bold in our preaching, we do so in a gentle fashion.

Many people feel isolated in our society. They feel like everyone is against them: the government, the police, the church, and in many cases even family. They may feel that they are being beat up on and have nowhere to turn. As Christians, we cannot be party to that kind of treatment. Rather, we need to stop and listen to them with love and gentleness, not rebuking them in anger and hostility. There is a time for tough love, but even that must be done with gentleness and self-control.

As with all the fruit of the Spirit, we must turn to the life of Christ for our example. If we look to men, we will be disappointed. Even the best of men fail to live up to the standard set by Christ.

SELF-CONTROL

If there is any specific fruit that we struggle with the most, it is self-control. The reason is that of the two sides of man, material and spiritual, the material is dominant. The material side is the side we currently live in. It is the side of here and now. We may recognize that the spiritual side has the long-term effect; but we are more interested in the moment.

Most of this life has to do with self-gratification. That feeling drives most of our decisions and desires, from the cradle to the grave. Babies cry when they are hungry, wet, tired, bored, or just want to be held. They learn early on that if they just put up enough of a fuss, they will get what they want. While speaking with a young drug addict, I asked why he did not get off drugs. The answer was that he liked them. He received instant gratification from drugs. Even though he knew that drugs were controlling his life and were the cause of most of his troubles, he continued to take them.

Addiction is a similar problem to self-gratification. Chemical addictions caused by drugs or alcohol can be broken only if the self-gratification issue is tackled at the same time. Many an addict has gone through rehab only to be back on drugs in a matter of days or weeks, because of the instantaneous gratification the drugs provided.

Consider now self-control. This is tough. It requires all our strength to fight not only the chemical dependency but also the lifestyle. It requires changing friends and all the things that were part of the addiction world. This is doubly complicated when you figure in the spiritual warfare aspect.[39] Nevertheless, self-control is required in all aspects of the Christian's life: the way we talk, the things we watch, the attitudes we display, and our thoughts. All must be under our self-control.

---

[39] See chapter 10.

CHAPTER 7

My Responsibilities to the Holy Spirit

While the believer is not perfected in this world, he still has a responsibility to be obedient to the teachings of Christ and the apostles. Jesus said, "Go therefore and make disciples of all the nations, baptizing them in the name of the Father and the Son and the Holy Spirit, teaching them to observe all that I commanded you; and lo, I am with you always, even to the end of the age" (Matt. 28:19–20). This includes obeying not just the big things but the little things as well. This means not just on Sunday but throughout the entire week. Many Christians have proclaimed that since they go to church on Sunday, they are doing just fine in this life, but that is not true! Jesus said, "teaching them to *obey all* that I commanded you" (Matthew 28:20, emphasis mine). The ability to obey Christ is not available to just anyone. We must understand that only a person who has received the indwelling of the Spirit has the ability to overcome the temptations and evils of this world.

Throughout the New Testament, there is a threefold division of relationships between men and God. These consist of (1) the Jew, who is under the old law, attempting to live his life consistent with

Old Testament Law; (2) the Gentile, or any non-Jew, following the ways of the world; and (3) the born-again believer. It is to the born-again believer in Corinth the apostle Paul writes, "Give no offence either to Jews, or to Greeks, or to the Church of God" (1 Cor. 10:32). The Jew relies on his relationship to God based on an old law; the Gentile (Greek) has no will to obey the teachings of Jesus; only the believer (church of God) has both the desire and ability (he has the indwelling of the Holy Spirit) to be obedient.

In the New Testament, we are given two very specific commands regarding our relationship with the Holy Spirit: (1) "Do not grieve the Holy Spirit of God" (Eph. 4:30), and (2) "Do not quench the Spirit" (1 Thess. 5:19 NASB).

"DO NOT GRIEVE THE HOLY SPIRIT OF GOD"

If, in fact, the Holy Spirit indwells the Christian, "with the purpose in view that the divine life should dominate all his thoughts, actions, and feelings rather than sin,"[40] then the presence of sin in the life of a Christian must surely grieve the Spirit. It is for this very reason that the apostle Paul wrote to the church in Ephesus: "And do not grieve the Holy Spirit of God, with whom you were sealed for the day of redemption. Get rid of all bitterness, rage and anger, brawling and slander, along with every form of malice. Be kind and compassionate to one another, forgiving each other, just as in Christ God forgave you" (Eph. 4:30–32). Here Paul gives the command "Do not grieve the Holy Spirit of God." He then states the reason why we are not to grieve the Spirit, "with whom you were sealed for the day of redemption." Finally, he enumerates those things that cause the Holy Spirit to grieve: "bitterness, rage and anger, brawling and slander, along with every form of malice." The apostle John also recognized how easy it is for us to disregard any effort the Spirit puts forth helping us to live the divine life, and so he too reminded us that our lives were to be sinless: "My dear children, I write these

---

[40] Chafer, *Systematic Theology*, VI, 234.

things to you so you will not sin" (1 John 2:1). Any sort of sin in our lives causes a separation between God and us. We cannot claim to be living a righteous life and yet continue to live in sin. "We know that anyone born of God does not continue to sin" (1 John 5:18). John also says, "But you know that he appeared so that he might take away our sins. *And in him is no sin*. No one who lives in him keeps on sinning. No one who continues to sin has either seen him or known him" (1 John 3:5–6; emphasis mine). Since God is without sin, His Spirit cannot function where sin exists, and so He grieves. Now this does not mean that we lose God's Spirit; "No one who is born of God will continue to sin, because God's seed remains in him" (1 John 3:9). Sin interrupts the ministry of the Spirit, but the Spirit remains. He cannot bring peace and comfort where sin flourishes. He cannot bring joy to a heart filled with guilt. So He strives with man to bring about an acknowledgement of guilt and a desire for repentance.

There are two steps required to find our way back to a Spirit-filled life: acknowledgement, and repentance. You will notice praying for forgiveness was not included. While it is not wrong to pray for forgiveness, it is not necessary. The New Testament teaches a single act brought about atonement for our sin, and that was the death of our Lord and Savior, Jesus Christ. He was the unspotted lamb offered up to God that our sins might be forgiven. However, even that only paved the way for us to receive forgiveness. Remember, when Peter was asked on the day of Pentecost, "What must we do to be saved?" His reply was, "Repent and be baptized, every one of you, in the name of Jesus Christ for the forgiveness of your sins" (Acts 2:38). For forgiveness to happen, we must first recognize our sin. Without acknowledgement of sin, there is nothing to forgive. This not only applies to the most recent convert, but to the oldest saint as well. Once we recognize our sin, we are in a position to do something about it—that is, repent. Acknowledgement comes from the mind, but repentance must come from the heart. While the literal meaning of repentance in the Greek is to have a "change of mind," this must be a sincere desire, motivated by true regret for the actions that leads to the need to repent. In substance abuse programs, the first step is for a person to acknowledge he or she has a problem. That, however, is not the cure. The cure comes from the heart-wrenching self-denial of the substance. The biblical story of the prodigal son comes to mind when Christians think of forgiveness. There was a father who had two sons. The youngest son decided he wanted his share of the estate so he could go live his life as he desired. After some time had gone by, broke, living in a pigpen, and eating slop, he came to the realization that his life was a mess. At this, he decided he would be better off back home as a servant than out on his own. This was step one, acknowledgement. He then returned home and said to his father, "Father, I have sinned against heaven and against you. I am no longer worthy to be called your son" (Luke 15:21). This was step two, repentance. At this, his father forgave him and restored him to his former place in the family. As Christians, we are like the prodigal son. We are members of the family of God, but we sin and go off to live life on our own. God does not disown us. He watches and waits patiently for us to open our eyes and recognize what we have done. When we are ready, we return home, turning from the wickedness that we had fallen into. He opens His arms and receives us back. He does not require that we ask for forgiveness. Acknowledgement and heartfelt repentance are all that is necessary. Asking for forgiveness is a human concern. As humans we expect a person to ask for forgiveness if he or she sins against us. But Christ has already forgiven us. He doesn't require us to ask over and over. What he wants, no, expects, is for us to recognize our sin, confess it, and then get back on the right track.

We see in scripture that the burden of repentance is on the one who sins; the burden of forgiveness lies with the one who has been sinned against. Consider these passages of scripture: "Be on your guard! If your brother sins, rebuke him; and if he repents, forgive him. And if he sins against you seven times a day, and returns to you seven times, saying, 'I repent,' forgive him" (Luke 17:3–4), and "If we confess our sins, He is faithful and righteous to forgive us our sins and to cleanse us from all unrighteousness" (1 John 1:9).

The second command regarding our relationship with the Spirit is even more serious than grieving the Spirit. When we grieve the Spirit, He is still active in our lives. But we can reach a point where we actually quench the Spirit. The NIV translation reads, "do not put out the Spirit's fire" (1 Thess. 5:19).

"DO NOT QUENCH THE SPIRIT"

The Greek word means to extinguish, put out, or restrain. The question is how does one go about extinguishing the Holy Spirit? The Spirit is the power of God in our lives. He is our guide, comforter, and lifeline to the Father. It is God's desire that we become sinless. In that regard, He sent his Son to be the atonement for our sin. When the Son left, He sent the Spirit to carry on His work in each of our individual lives. John the Baptist said that Jesus would baptize us with the Holy Spirit and with fire (Matt. 3:11). That fire is the foundation of our lives on this earth; it is the process of sanctification. Consider the prophesy of Zechariah:

> "In the whole land," declares the LORD,
> "two-thirds will be struck down and perish;
> yet one-third will be left in it.
> This third I will bring into the fire;
> I will refine them like silver
> and test them like gold.
> They will call on my name
> and I will answer them;
> I will say, 'They are my people,'
> and they will say, 'The LORD is our God.'" (Zech. 13:8–9)

Throughout history, fire has been used, both physically and symbolically, as a purification agent. God refines us through the Holy Spirit. The prophet Isaiah said, "See, I have refined you, though not as silver; I have tested you in the furnace of affliction" (Isa. 48:10).

The apostle Peter describes it this way: "In this you greatly rejoice, though now for a little while you may have had to suffer grief in all kinds of trials. These have come so that your faith—of greater worth than gold, which perishes even though refined by fire—may be proved genuine and may result in praise, glory and honor when Jesus Christ is revealed" (1 Pet. 1:6–7).

When we as born-again believers speak or act in such a way as to prevent the Spirit from fulfilling His purpose in our lives, we are quenching Him. We do this when we turn away from the teachings of the Word, from prayer, from the fellowship of believers. But it is more than just a turning away: that grieves the Spirit. This is a direct, purposeful attempt to separate ourselves from all the joys and blessings we held as believers. This is not a single act. It is a process over time. It starts when we begin to find things outside of Christ that become more important than Christ Himself: these things are most often innocent in nature.

In the parable of the sower, Jesus spoke with His disciples regarding this issue.

> "Listen! A farmer went out to sow his seed. As he was scattering the seed, some fell along the path, and the birds came and ate it up. Some fell on rocky places, where it did not have much soil. It sprang up quickly, because the soil was shallow. But when the sun came up, the plants were scorched, and they withered because they had no root. Other seed fell among thorns, which grew up and choked the plants, so that they did not bear grain. Still other seed fell on good soil. It came up, grew and produced a crop, multiplying thirty, sixty, or even a hundred times." Then Jesus said, "He who has ears to hear, let him hear." (Mark 4:3–9 NIV)

The second seed is the one we are most concerned with here. In my years in ministry I have come across a number of individuals who, when faced with adversity, instead of turning to the Spirit for help and comfort, have become disappointed with God and turned away from Him. Their faith was shallow and weak. This is one of the reasons why being in a mentoring relationship with a more mature person in the fellowship of believers is so important. Such a person can help direct us back to the Spirit, and to prayer, and to the Word!

Men often get caught up in work. A man's job is his identity. His importance and his status in the community are determined by what he does for a living. An assumption is made that if he has an important job and makes a lot of money, he is a good person. For example, the owner of a construction company is held in higher esteem than the laborer who works for him. The fact of the matter is that the laborer may be far more righteous, caring, and spiritual than the owner. Even though they may start at the same point in baptism, if one begins to let the stress and importance of the job take him away from family, church, and prayer, he is on the path of eventual denial.

Women are no less subject to this disaster. While women tend less to be identified by work, they are identified by relationships. They are more likely to place a greater emphasis on relationships than a man does. Many workplace romances start with a simple smile or a flattering comment. This downhill spiral may begin innocently but often leads to denial, lying, anger, hostility. Such actions then lead to a separation of one's relationship with Christ, and ultimately not only denial, which can be recovered from, but an utter refusal to have anything to do with Christ! At this point, the person enters into a different position than simple denial. The writer of Hebrews puts it this way: "It is impossible for those who have once been enlightened, who have tasted the heavenly gift, who have shared in the Holy Spirit, who have tasted the goodness of the word of God and the powers of the coming age, if they fall away, to be brought back to repentance, because to their loss they are crucifying the Son of God all over again and subjecting him to public disgrace" (Heb. 6:4–6 NIV). The term used in the scripture for this is *blasphemy*.

THE ISSUE OF BLASPHEMY

One of the things we are taught to obey is recorded in the writings of Mark: "Truly I say to you, all sins shall be forgiven the sons of men, and whatever blasphemies they utter; but whoever blasphemes against the Holy Spirit never has forgiveness, but is guilty of an eternal sin" (Mark 3:28–29). Blasphemy is speaking out against, or slandering, the name of God, whether as the Father, the Son, or the Holy Spirit. This is also referred to by many as the "unforgiveable sin."

As Christians, we hold in high esteem the very being of God; whether of God the Father, God the Son, or God the Holy Spirit. We recognize that it is not enough to "talk the talk"; we must also "walk the walk." This means in our words as well as action. Blaspheme is the opposite extreme. When we slander the name of God, we seek to deny completely who and what He is. This is the action of one who has utterly no desire for a relationship with God. Blasphemy is "a deliberate and direct attack upon the honor of God with intent to insult him."[41]

The *New Dictionary of Theology* says, "Blasphemy ... is no specific sin, such as denial of the Spirit's divinity, but that disposition of deliberate hostility to the power of God actualized through the person of the Trinity which precludes a person's contrition and repentance."[42]

Consider Hymenaeus and Alexander. While we know very little about Hymenaeus and Alexander, we do know they were referred to as blasphemers by the apostle Paul (1 Tim. 1:20). The apparent reason for this reference was that they denied the future resurrection of Christ (2 Tim. 2:17–18), claiming the resurrection had already taken place and that by making that claim they were destroying the faith of others.

When we think of blasphemy, we must also consider the issue of conscience. God created us with a conscience to help us recognize

---

[41] *"Blasphemy"*, *New Catholic Encyclopedia*, vol. 2, 606-607.
[42] Ferguson and Wright, *New Dictionary of Theology*, 105.

right from wrong. This is separate from the Holy Spirit. Everyone has a conscience; only believers in Jesus Christ have the indwelling of the Holy Spirit. In today's high-tech world, we might think of conscience as a firewall for our minds. Anti-virus/malware software works to prevent our computers from acquiring instructions that might be destructive; our conscience functions in much the same fashion. When you are about to do something wrong, your conscience might cause you to recognize it is wrong and rethink what you are about to do; it helps prevent you from lying, cheating, or stealing. Whether there is a specific law against what you are doing, your conscience operates on a moral, ethical basis.

A seared conscience happens when you repeatedly fail to listen to your conscience. Over time, what you may have considered to be morally reprehensible, you may willingly accept. Christians are susceptible to this when they listen to culture and ignore the teachings of Christ. After a while, they accept culture's morality and turn a deaf ear to the things of God. Paul addresses this in his letter to the church in Rome:

> For it is not those who hear the law who are righteous in God's sight, but it is those who obey the law who will be declared righteous. (Indeed, when Gentiles, who do not have the law, do by nature things required by the law, they are a law for themselves, even though they do not have the law, since they show that the requirements of the law are written on their hearts, their consciences also bearing witness, and their thoughts now accusing, now even defending them.) (Rom. 2:13–15)

Consider also,

> Woe to those who call evil good and good evil, who put darkness for light and light for darkness, who put bitter for sweet and sweet for bitter. (Isa. 5:20)

And,

> You have wearied the LORD with your words. "How have we wearied him?" you ask. By saying, "All who do evil are good in the eyes of the LORD, and he is pleased with them" or "Where is the God of justice?" (Mal. 2:17)

CHAPTER 8

Being Filled with the Spirit

Eleven times the New Testament refers to being filled with the Holy Spirit. Paul actually commands that we be filled with the Spirit: "And do not get drunk on wine, for it is a dissipation, but be filled with the Spirit" (Eph. 5:18). What does it mean to "be filled with the Holy Spirit, and how is that different from receiving the gift of the Holy Spirit and spiritual gifts?

WHAT DOES "FILLED WITH THE HOLY SPIRIT" MEAN?

For many Christians, having received the gift of the Spirit is all they feel they need or want, but this is a very unhealthy view of the Christian life. Repeatedly we are told about the joy and power to overcome life's troubles, but so many fail to experience that joy and power. To understand this, we must consider the word *filled*. In the Greek it is a constant overflowing. It is not a once in a while or occasional experience. As a fly fisherman, there have been occasions when I was blessed to fish a mountain spring-fed creek. No matter what time of the year, the creek was running with an unlimited supply of water from the spring. This is not like the tail waters of a reservoir, where the flow is controlled by the Corps of Engineers and turned on and off. Spring creeks are continuously supplied. For the Christian this means that we should be filled to overflowing with the joy and power of the Spirit: we should not display the power of the Spirit occasionally or just when we are expressing joy in a worship service. The Christian who is not experiencing the Spirit-filled life regularly is surely a disappointment to God, who expects each of us to experience His Spirit to the maximum.

In his book, *The Holy Spirit*,[43] Billy Graham references an old Welsh revival prayer:

> Fill me, Holy Spirit, fill me,
> More than fullness I would know;
> I am smallest of Thy vessels,
> Yet, I much can overflow.

Time and again, as a pastor, I have been asked, "If I experience periods of doubt, sorrow, or even depression, does that mean I am not filled with the Spirit?" The answer is an unqualified no! Sometimes God might use these feelings to draw attention to a specific problem. It might also be a way of helping us to express compassion toward someone else who is experiencing troubles in his or her own life. Clients often tell their counselors, "If you haven't experienced [fill in the blank] you can't help me." So we ought not confuse such feelings with a lack of the fullness of the Spirit. Having said that, if such feelings begin to dominate your life, you might want to seek help to understand what is causing these feelings.

IS SPEAKING IN TONGUES A SIGN
OF BEING SPIRIT FILLED?

Speaking in tongues is a gift of the Spirit, but just because someone has spoken in a tongue does not mean he or she is

---

[43] Graham, *The Holy Spirit*, 145.

necessarily filled with the Spirit. Different groups refer to the experience as being "baptized in the Spirit" or "the second blessing of the Spirit." The Assemblies of God, for instance, place great importance on speaking in tongues: "We believe the baptism in the Holy Spirit with the initial physical evidence of speaking in other tongues is the promise of the Father to every Christian who desires the experience."[44] These groups see this experience much the same way others view the basic filling of the Holy Spirit, with or without the experience of a charismatic gift such as speaking in a tongue. One of the issues that the Assemblies have to deal with is making sure that those who have not experienced speaking in tongues are not viewed as second-class citizens: "In the Assemblies of God we believe the Spirit is at work in all Christians, whether they have been baptized in the Spirit or not. God can also use and does use Christians who for one reason or another have not received the baptism experience. We must never depreciate their ministry. Yet we recognize the baptism in the Holy Spirit will make one's life and ministry even more effective."[45]

THE FIRST FILLING WITH THE SPIRIT

To fully appreciate the meaning of being filled with the Spirit, we must look at the first Christian experience of the Spirit's filling. This occurred fifty days after the resurrection of Jesus. Today we celebrate this as Pentecost.[46] It also took place ten days after the ascension of Jesus. We find it recorded for us in Acts 2:1–47.

The disciples gathered behind locked doors for fear of what the authorities might do to them. All of a sudden there was a loud noise like a rushing wind. We might describe it today like the sound of a tornado! One can only imagine how frightening that was. Then,

---

[44] https://ag.org/Beliefs/Topics-Index/Holy-Spirit-Baptism-Baptism-in-the-Holy-Spirit

[45] Ibid.

[46] *Pentecost* is the Greek word for fifty.

what is described as tongues of fire came down from heaven and settled on each of them. This was the Holy Spirit, Himself, filling them. The result of this was that they totally overcame their fear, and they began speaking in languages that they had never learned. Together they went out into the temple and began testifying about Jesus being the Christ, the Son of God.

While some read this as an explanation of the filling of the Holy Spirit, others, as we have noted, believe that each and every believer should experience exactly the same thing, and since the disciples spoke in "tongues," so should we. However, the apostle Paul describes speaking in tongues as a spiritual gift (1 Cor. 12:10). This is not something that every Christian receives.

HOW CAN I BE FILLED WITH THE SPIRIT?

Some people say, "Just believe!" Others say, "Pray for the filling." Mere belief is not the same as "having faith." James said, "You believe that God is one; you do well. Even the demons believe—and shudder" (James 2:19). Having faith, however, means acting on that belief. While we are saved by grace, through faith (Eph. 2:8–9), faith demands a changed life. Being filled with the Spirit is demonstrative of the Holy Spirit working continually in the life of the believer. If one wants, and expects, to be filled with the Spirit, it would seem that in addition to not quenching the Spirit, and not grieving the Spirit, one must "walk in the Spirit." Paul writes to the Galatian church: "But I say, walk by the Spirit, and you will not carry out the desire of the flesh" (Gal. 5:16).

The Greek text has the word *walk* as present tense. This can be translated, "continue walking." The meaning here is that the Galatians were walking in the Spirit, and Paul encourages them to keep it up. While there are a number of scripture passages where charismatic gifts are enjoined with the filling of the Spirit, it does not appear that this is an absolute. What that means is, whether one is displaying some miraculous gift or not, he or she may still be filled with the Spirit. This obviously goes against the teachings of some Catholic and Pentecostal groups.

The apostle John is very distinct in his first letter regarding walking in the Light (or in the Spirit). The whole implication in that letter is that if we are in a right relationship with God, our lives will be demonstrations of Spirit fullness. If you remove the Pentecostal element from the teaching, then the filling of the Spirit and walking in the Spirit are inextricably intertwined.

DIFFERENCE BETWEEN THE INDWELLING AND FILLING

Many people have questioned the difference between the indwelling of the Spirit, whom we receive at baptism, and the filling of the Spirit spoken of throughout the New Testament.

The indwelling, as we have already reasoned, comes at the time of Christian baptism. It does not come at just any baptism, but only at Christian baptism. The apostle Paul tells of a group of believers at Ephesus (Acts 19:1–7). He asked them, "Have your received the Holy Spirit since you believed?"

They answered, "No."

So Paul asked, "Then what baptism did you receive?"

"John's baptism," they replied.

John's baptism was a baptism of repentance, not a baptism in the name of Jesus. Therefore, Paul placed his hands on them and baptized them in the name of Jesus, and they began speaking in tongues.[47]

The indwelling of the Spirit is the full manifestation of the Holy Spirit within our body. Every baptized believer in Jesus Christ has equally received the Holy Spirit.

The "filling of the Spirit" is a different matter. While we all possess the full manifestation of the Spirit equally, His work within

---

[47] This was a visible sign that they had now, in fact, received the Holy Spirit.

us is not equal. We find references to specific persons in both the Old and New Testaments who were "filled with the Spirit."

A term frequently used in the Old Testament is, "the Spirit came upon …" This is an equivalent expression to "filled with the Spirit." A study of the Old Testament would reveal that the Spirit came upon a number of individuals, including Samson, Balaam, Saul, the prophet Azariah, and Ezekiel, as well as numerous others. In each case, the Spirit came upon them that they might accomplish some specific purpose.

In the New Testament, we also find numerous persons, such as John the Baptist (Luke 1:13–15), Peter (Acts 4:8), and Paul (Acts 13:9), all being "filled with the Spirit," but their purpose was much broader in nature. Typically, they were to perform ministry of a much broader in scale. For example, in Acts 3:1–10, the story is told of Peter and John, who were on their way to the temple to pray, when they encountered a crippled man begging for money. Both Peter and John looked at him, and Peter said, "Silver or gold I do not have, but what I have I give you. In the name of Jesus Christ of Nazareth, walk." At that, the man, who had been crippled from birth, jumped to his feet and began praising God. When the people saw this, they were amazed. Peter then used this opportunity to testify about Jesus.

When we give our lives totally over to Christ and are fully absorbed in Him, we too can experience the true filling of the Holy Spirit.

CHAPTER 9

The Opposing Forces

WHAT/WHO ARE THE OPPOSING FORCES?

While God fully expects the church to work with the fullness of the Holy Spirit, it is not without opposition. From the beginning of time, man has been forced to contend with the temptation to veer away from righteousness, obedience, holiness, and truth. When Adam and Eve walked in the Garden of Eden, they were commanded not to eat from the tree of the knowledge of good and evil (Gen. 2:17). This was the introduction of the force of evil in the world.

Even the nonspiritual world realizes the forces of evil in the world. In 1959 a movie was released titled *The World, the Flesh, and the Devil*. It starred Harry Belafonte, Inger Stevens, and Mel Ferrer. The short story is that Belafonte is trapped in a mine he was inspecting. After his would-be rescuers give up, he digs himself out, only to find that the world as he knows it has come to an end. He wanders around and ends up in New York City. Here he finds he is not alone; Inger Stevens comes on the scene. She and Belafonte become close friends. In time, they find out there are other survivors in Europe. Sometime later, Mel Ferrer arrives by boat and takes a shine to Inger. Hostilities grow between Belafonte and Ferrer. So here is the plot: even in a postapocalyptic world, three people cannot get along peacefully. The movie ends with the line "Not the End: The Beginning." I will leave it to your imagination to figure out what that means.

Since that time of Adam and Eve, mankind has had to contend with three powerful forces—the world, the flesh, and the devil.

THE WORLD

The apostle John alluded to this battle in his first epistle: "For everything in the world—the cravings of sinful man, the lust of his eyes and the boasting of what he has and does—comes not from the Father but from the world" (1 John 2:16). Here we see the full effect of the infamous quote from Pogo, "We have met the enemy, and he is us."[48] Humanity brings upon itself all of the ills and evil it faces. This is not to say there is no outside influence; that would be to deny the scriptures, for both Old and New Testaments reference the outside force of evil. However, that force only operates when men and women choose to give in to it.

The realization that Satan has been given, by God, control over the present age is a truth that is not often heard: persons in this day and age fail to recognize that the whole world is under the domination of Satan. Several Greek words used in the New Testament are translated world and have widely varied meanings: ai=wvn (aeon), a reference to a period of time, an age; koumevnh (kumena), a reference to the inhabited earth; and kovsmoV (cosmos), often referring to the "present condition of human affairs," in alienation from and opposition to God, generally has a negative connotation. It is this last form that is used most often (186 times) in the New Testament. We should note that it is this world that Jesus says Satan is the prince over: "Now judgment is upon this world; now the ruler of this world shall be cast out" (John 12:31); "I will not speak with you much longer, for the prince of this world

---

[48] http://www.thwink.org/sustain/tools/images/PogoEarthDay Poster1970.jpg.

is coming. He has no hold on me" (John 14:30); and "in regard to judgment, because the prince of this world now stands condemned" (John 16:11).

The early church that the apostle James writes to apparently failed to understand that it could not be "friends" with the world without being "enemies" of God: "You adulterous people, don't you know that friendship with the world is hatred toward God? Anyone who chooses to be a friend of the world becomes an enemy of God" (James 4:4).

We live in a part of an orderly, well-defined, and regulated cosmic system, called the world. It consists of not only a material realm, but a spiritual realm as well. While we only see the material side, the spiritual side is just as real. While we live in the world, we are not to become polluted by it: "Religion that God our Father accepts as pure and faultless is this: to look after orphans and widows in their distress and to keep oneself from being polluted by the world" (James 1:27).

We face numerous problems in the world today. We tend to think of these problems mostly from a material perspective: pollution, climate change, nuclear proliferation, war in the Middle East, hunger, and poverty. Some of these problems are man-made and others are the natural cause of nature. However, there is another whole list of problems fabricated by man. These are such things as hostility, discrimination, deceit, adultery, riots, drugs, and general wickedness. These things are not caused by forces of nature but the evil of mankind.

From the last half of the nineteenth century through most of the twentieth century, the church kept much of the wickedness in check. However, in the 1970s there was a major change in attitudes to organized religion. New Age religion began to sweep the nation with chants such as "Let go: let God." The idea was that we did not need to focus on God; just let Him do His thing. "I'm okay; you're okay" was another common claim. This claim said, "No matter what you do, how you act or think, I will not judge you. The same applies to me, and you must not judge me." Another was, "If it feels good, do it!" This was one of the most destructive claims. It took away all reason and logic and put everything into the realm of feeling. Bind the mind and free the heart. However, a completely free heart takes away fear of God and the law. This is the opposite of conscience.

Much of the New Age movement focused on Eastern religions such as Buddhism and Hinduism. The concept of "karma" came from these religions. Karma is the idea that man's nature affects his future. For example, "Good intent and good deed contribute to good karma and future happiness, while bad intent and bad deed contribute to bad karma and future suffering."[49] The idea of karma affects in a major way how we think about free will. If someone rapes, robs, or kills someone else, was it his or her karma that was the cause, and the action was beyond the control of the individual? It was during this same period that it became popular to claim that each person is a product of his or her environment. Individual actions should not be held against people since those actions should have been anticipated.

Today, a number of churches have bought into a smorgasbord of ideas on how to deal with the empty hearts of those in their congregations. We base most of these ideas on human philosophies. The problem with this is that these philosophies deal with the symptoms, not the problem itself. It is like the pain-relieving device called the "willow curve"; while it may temporarily relieve the pain, it does nothing to deal with the root cause of the pain.

An example of this is the whole gay rights issue. The church from its inception has taught all sexual acts outside of marriage were immoral and sinful (1 Cor. 7:1–5; Rom. 1:26–27). Until the mid twentieth century, this remained the primary teaching on sex in the church, schools, and most Christian homes. However, in the 1980s, the AIDS epidemic began almost exclusively among homosexual men.[50] In an effort to stem the epidemic, homosexual men were encouraged to "come out of the closet" and seek medical

---

[49] https://en.wikipedia.org/wiki/Karma.
[50] https://www.aids.gov/hiv-aids-basics/hiv-aids-101/aids-timeline/index.html.

help. Watching young men die of such a horrible disease was unbearable for most of society. It quickly became popular to say that the homosexual relationship was not simply a choice; but rather, it was the way God made them! This immoral act has morphed from sin to simple biological function. As homosexuality (followed by the lesbian relationship) became publicly acceptable, the issues of discrimination jumped to the forefront. Now the entire gay, lesbian, bisexual, transgender (GLBT) community has begun demanding civil rights! The result of this has been that 96-plus percent of the American population is being dictated to by less than 4 percent of the population.[51]

The saddest part of this is that even in the church we find whole denominations being split over these issues: issues that only came about because we let the world dictate morality to the church, instead of the church encouraging biblical morality in an immoral world.

It has been said of the church in the twentieth century, "There is not enough church in the world, and too much world in the church." When we turn our eyes away from Christ and look to the world to solve our spiritual problems, we will be greatly disappointed and in the end eternally lost! The apostle John states it this way: "Do not love the world or anything in the world. If anyone loves the world, the love of the Father is not in him. For everything in the world—the cravings of sinful man, the lust of his eyes and the boasting of what he has and does—comes not from the Father but from the world. The world and its desires pass away, but the man who does the will of God lives forever" (1 John 2:15–17).

THE FLESH

The human body is made up of three parts; material, soul, and spirit. Several Greek words deal with the human body. The two we are most interested in are swma (soma) and *savrx* (sarx). While soma deals with the body in a physical sense, sarx infers a more complete

---

[51] https://carm.org/percent-population-homosexual.

definition since it deals with the whole of humanity: body, soul, and spirit. Consider John 1:14: "And the Word was made flesh [sarx]." This speaks of the incarnate Christ. He came not just in a material body of flesh and bone, but a fully human body of flesh and bone, soul, and spirit. Therefore, we can see that sarx is more inclusive than soma: it includes the totality of a human being. The International Standard Bible Encyclopedia (ISBE) says this about the word *sarx*: "Human nature, being inferior to the spiritual, is to be in subjection to it. If man refuses to be under this higher law, and as a free agent permits the lower nature to gain an ascendancy over the spirit, the 'flesh' becomes a revolting force (Gen. 6:3, 12; John 1:13; Rom. 7:14; Col. 3:1–3; Col. 2:18; 1 John 2:16). Thus, the fleshly or carnal mind (i.e., a mind in subjection to carnal nature) is opposed to the Divine spirit, who alone is a sufficient corrective."[52]

Now, for a moment, permit me to dive into a rabbit hole and deal with a very controversial issue: Does the sin of Adam make us all sinners from birth, or is it our personal sin that condemns us? I only raise this issue for purpose of thought, not that we will answer the question to the satisfaction of all. But it must be considered in context with the flesh, since sarx is frequently used in the New Testament in reference to the carnal nature of man.

There is a belief among a number of different religious groups that because Adam sinned, that sin is passed from generation to generation through birth. Therefore, everyone from the time of Adam is automatically a sinner. It is for this reason that these groups generally baptize infants.

The other side is that man becomes a sinner through personal sin. When the carnal nature of man is not subordinate to the higher nature, sin occurs. This is a choice each individual has; it is known as free will. Therefore, there is no need for infant baptism, since infants only know eating, sleeping, and other bodily functions. The idea of an infant knowingly (free will) not subordinating his or her carnal nature to the higher nature is without any justification whatsoever.

---

[52] Knutson, F. B. *International Standard Bible Encyclopedia. http://www. internationalstandardbible.com/F/flesh.html,*

Let's look at some scripture references to help show this carnal side of man: "For the flesh [sarx] sets its desire against the Spirit, and the Spirit against the flesh [sarx]; for these are in opposition to one another, so that you may not do the things that you please" (Gal. 5:17). This clearly shows the carnal nature and its opposition to one's higher nature. To the church in Corinth the apostle Paul writes, "Do you not know that your bodies [soma] are temples of the Holy Spirit, who is in you, whom you have received from God? You are not your own" (1 Cor. 6:19). Here Paul says even our physical/material bodies belong to God, for they are His temples.

The apostle Paul's letter to the church in Rome clearly contrasts the difference between two natures (Rom. 7:14–17). All men face this struggle when they enter into the realm of salvation. Once saved, I have a new, higher nature based on having been cleansed of my sins and having received the Holy Spirit. However, this does not mean the old sinful nature has been annihilated; quite the contrary. The sinful nature has now come into competition with the higher nature. Which wins out? Ultimately, it is the higher nature, but it appears from Paul's writings that it is not without a fight (Rom. 7:15–21). Paul also answers the question in his letter to the Galatians: "But I say, walk by the Spirit, and you will not carry out the desire of the flesh [sarx]. For the flesh [sarx] sets its desire against the Spirit, and the Spirit against the flesh [sarx]; for these are in opposition to one another, so that you may not do the things that you please" (Gal. 5:16–17 NASB). The answer, it appears, is not just having the Holy Spirit but walking or living in the Spirit. We have the assurance of total victory over the flesh if we walk in the Spirit.

The apostle John writes to this issue as well, using light and darkness; light is the Holy Spirit, darkness is the way of the world or our sinful nature:

> Dear friends, I am not writing you a new command but an old one, which you have had since the beginning. This old command is the message you have heard. Yet I am writing you a new command; its

truth is seen in him and you, because the darkness is passing and the true light is already shining. Anyone who claims to be in the light but hates his brother is still in the darkness. Whoever loves his brother lives in the light, and there is nothing in him to make him stumble. But whoever hates his brother is in the darkness and walks around in the darkness; he does not know where he is going, because the darkness has blinded him. (1 John 2:7–11)

THE DEVIL

After more than thirty years of ministry, I never cease to be amazed at how many churchgoers believe in a personal savior but not in a personal devil. Yet, any serious and attentive reading of the Sacred Text will disclose two facts, namely: (1) that Satan is as real of a being as any other character depicted in the Bible, and (2) that, though limited in what he can do because of divine constraint, he wages an unceasing and unrelenting warfare against those who are saved. In counseling the newly baptized, it is vitally important to introduce them to the topic of Satanology. The unsaved have little to fear from Satan since they reside in his kingdom already: "For he has rescued us from the dominion of darkness and brought us into the kingdom of the Son he loves" (Col. 1:13), and he is their father: "You belong to your father, the devil, and you want to carry out your father's desire" (John 8:44a). However, to the saved, "*Your enemy* the devil prowls around like a roaring lion looking for someone to devour" (1 Pet. 5:8; emphasis mine). Having denounced Satan and having received the Holy Spirit, we become an enemy of Satan. Satan will do all in his power to hurt Jesus Christ, and the most obvious way is to turn around those who are weak in the Spirit and cause them to go back to their sinful natures.

Satan does not have unlimited power. He is constrained by

God.[53] Part of this is that Satan cannot violate man's free will, any more than God chooses not to violate man's free will. It might be said that man's free will is sacred. Christians must understand that while Satan is a powerful adversary, he is not as powerful as the Holy Spirit: "You, dear children, are from God and have overcome them, because the one who is in you is greater than the one who is in the world" (1 John 4:4). It is this fact that should guide the believer in all his actions. The only power Satan really has over the saved is that which the individual allows. This is not to say, however, that we can take Satan frivolously. He is a powerful enemy: "The Scriptures declare that Satan is king over two realms: that of fallen spirits whose number is legion (Mark 5:9, 15; Luke 8:30), and that of the *cosmos*."[54] The apostle Paul makes the statement that Satan is "the god of this age" (2 Cor. 4:4) and that he has authority of the demons (Matt. 12:22–30). This being the case, we cannot fight against such a potentate on our own. This is where the Holy Spirit steps in. His authority and power exceed that of Satan.

Satan is not omnipotent, nor omniscient, nor omnipresent. Unlike God, Satan is not all-powerful. For example, one day the angels came to present themselves before God, and Satan came with them. Satan got into a debate with God about Job. Satan believed he could do things to Job to get him to curse God, but he needed God's permission. Finally, God consented and said, "Very well, then, everything he has is in your hands, but on the man himself do not lay a finger" (Job 1:12). Satan was limited in what he could do to Job.[55] He cannot do anything to us that God does not allow; he cannot be in more than one place at a time. Unlike God, Satan has limited knowledge. God knows all that has happened and all that will happen in the future. Satan only knows what has happened or is happening. If Satan were omniscient, he would know that he has already lost the battle with God, and he would know who will ultimately accept Christ and those who won't. However, he does not

---

[53] Consider the story of Job, especially Job 1:1–12.
[54] Chafer, vol. 2, 113.
[55] Read the entire book of Job for the full story.

know those things, and so he continues to war against God in the hopes he will ultimately win the battle. Finally, unlike God, Satan, being a created being, is limited to one place at a time. It is for this reason he uses his demons to harass, deceive, and destroy the lives of people. He especially desires to harass the new believer. This is when the believer is most susceptible to being drawn back into the kingdom of darkness and out of the light.

In C. S. Lovett's book *Dealing with the Devil*,[56] he makes the biblical case that Satan is real and after believers, but that this is spiritual, not physical; he attacks us primarily through our thoughts and minds. Lovett's mantra is "Resist the devil and he will flee from you" (James 4:7). This is where our only hope for a steadfast life in Christ lies: our unrelenting dependence on the Holy Spirit and resistance against Satan.

THE ISSUE OF SPIRITUAL WARFARE

No study of the Holy Spirit would be complete without a brief understanding of angels, demons, and their interaction with humans. There are more than a few Christians who believe in the Holy Spirit, and even that there is an Unholy Spirit, but refuse to believe in the whole issue of spiritual warfare. The very idea of being inhabited by demons is repulsive to them. Nevertheless, let us look at the truth of the matter.

We divide angels into two major classifications: (1) the unfallen angels and (2) the fallen angels. Both started out as beings created by God: "Praise him, all his angels, praise him, all his heavenly hosts ... Let them praise the name of the LORD, for he commanded and they were created" (Ps. 148:2–5); "For by him all things were created: things in heaven and on earth, visible and invisible, whether thrones or powers or rulers or authorities; all things were created by him and for him" (Col. 1:16). The word *angel* (Gr. *angelos*) simply means messenger. There is no high, holy meaning in and of the word

---

[56] Available from Amazon.com.

itself. The word is sometimes used of (1) human messengers: "And in the same way was not Rahab the harlot also justified by works, when she received the messengers (Gr. angelos) and sent them out by another way" (James 2:25) and (2) the departed spirits of those who have died: "And they said to her, 'You are out of your mind!' But she kept insisting that it was so. And they kept saying, 'It is his angel'" (Acts 12:15). To understand this reference, we must note that James, the brother of John, had been taken into custody by Herod, and then put to death by the sword. Peter was then taken into custody. When he showed up at the door, the disciples all assumed he too had been put to death, and it was his angel who stood before them. However, we should also note this is not justification for claiming that all dead spirits become angels (as is a common belief today). Similarly, there is no justification for the idea that the spirits of the evil dead all become demons.

Three times in scripture we find reference to the fall of Satan. First in the Old Testament, in Isaiah 14:12: "How you have fallen from heaven, O morning star, son of the dawn! You have been cast down to the earth, you who once laid low the nations!" Then in the New Testament we have Jesus making reference to the fall of Satan, in Luke 10:18: "He replied, 'I saw Satan fall like lightning from heaven.'" Both references appear to refer to the original fall. This takes place prior to Adam and Eve in the garden (Gen. 3:1ff).

The third reference, and the most descriptive for our needs, comes to us from the writings of the apostle John. In Jesus's "Revelation," He relates the story of the fall of Satan, or the devil, and his angels (Rev. 12:7–11). This is the apparent beginning of what will climax with Armageddon, which is the final battle between good and evil, the end of time, victory of good over evil, and the general end of the world. Prior to this time, Satan had been given power over the earth: "Again, the devil took him to a very high mountain and showed him all the kingdoms of the world and their splendor. 'All this I will give you,' he said, 'if you will bow down and worship me'" (Matt. 4:8–9). Those angels who fell with Satan appear to be in two classes: (1) those who are in chains until a time to be released by God:

"And the angels who did not keep their positions of authority but abandoned their own home—these he has kept in darkness, bound with everlasting chains for judgment on the great Day" (Jude 1:6); and (2) those who are loose (demons?) to do Satan's bidding at the present time.

In the Gospels, it is apparent that Jesus was well aware of demons and their ability to inhabit both people and animals. Let's look at several passages of scripture that demonstrate this.

Shortly after Jesus selected His first disciples, He was in Galilee and "his fame spread throughout all Syria, and they brought him all the sick, those afflicted with various diseases and pains, those oppressed by demons, epileptics, and paralytics, and he healed them" (Matt. 4:24 ESV).

One day at Peter's house, Jesus healed Peter's mother-in-law, who had a fever. "That evening they brought to him many who were oppressed by demons, and he cast out the spirits with a word and healed all who were sick" (Matt. 8:16 ESV).

Another time,

> [When Jesus came] to the country of the Gadarenes, two demon-possessed men met him, coming out of the tombs, so fierce that no one could pass that way. And behold, they cried out, "What have you to do with us, O Son of God? Have you come here to torment us before the time?" Now a herd of many pigs was feeding at some distance from them, and the demons begged him, saying, "If you cast us out, send us away into the herd of pigs." And he said to them, "Go." So they came out and went into the pigs, and behold, the whole herd rushed down the steep bank into the sea and drowned in the waters. (Matt. 8:28–32 ESV)

> And God was doing extraordinary miracles by the hands of Paul, so that even handkerchiefs or aprons

that had touched his skin were carried away to the sick, and their diseases left them and the evil spirits came out of them. (Acts 19:11–12 ESV)

There are over thirty verses in the New Testament dealing with Jesus or one of the apostles casting out demons. The only way someone can deny that demons truly exist is to say that Jesus, the apostles, and the people of the day were too stupid to recognize what was happening. This would be a denial of Christ, His existence, and the entire New Testament. Only an atheist would dare to make such a claim, and that claim does not falsify the testimony of scripture. The historical correctness of the Bible has been shown repeatedly.[57]

The apostle Paul also attested to belief in the conflict between humans and demons. In his letter to the church in Ephesus, he wrote:

> Finally, be strong in the Lord and in the strength of his might. Put on the whole armor of God, that you may be able to stand against the schemes of the devil. For we do not wrestle against flesh and blood, but against the rulers, against the authorities, against the cosmic powers over this present darkness, against the spiritual forces of evil in the heavenly places. Therefore, take up the whole armor of God, that you may be able to withstand in the evil day, and having done all, to stand firm. Stand therefore, having fastened on the belt of truth, and having put on the breastplate of righteousness, and, as shoes for your feet, having put on the readiness given by the gospel of peace. In all circumstances take up the shield of faith, with which you can extinguish all the flaming darts of the evil one; and take the helmet of salvation, and the sword of the Spirit, which is the word of God, praying at all times in the Spirit, with

---

[57] Read *Evidence that Demands a Verdict* by Josh McDowell.

all prayer and supplication. To that end keep alert with all perseverance, making supplication for all the saints and also for me, that words may be given to me in opening my mouth boldly to proclaim the mystery of the gospel. (Eph. 6:10–20 ESV)

In addition to scripture, we have the testimony of the church. Church history has testified throughout regarding spiritual warfare. Much has been written about angels, both unfallen and fallen: "The writer of the *Shepherd of Hermas* actually envisioned two angels influencing each person. One is an angel of righteousness, fostering the good. Opposed to this is an angel of wickedness, who prompts its person toward evil."[58] In the early church, there was also interest in demon possession: "Believers in the early church experienced the reality of the spiritual realm vividly and constantly. For many, their entire earthly pilgrimage was devoted to repelling the onslaughts of evil spirits."[59] One of the early church fathers, Athanasius, wrote *The Life of St. Antony*.[60] There he told of how Satan himself had viciously attacked Antony repeatedly but to no avail.

To understand the belief in demons throughout church history, one has only to look at medieval architecture. Churches were often adorned with holy angels as well as demonic figures. This did not come about simply as a figment of someone's imagination. Even myths and legends have been shown to have validity in history.

In the twentieth and twenty-first centuries, many have developed a sense of arrogance that says they are smarter than anyone else in history was and understand the psychological as well as physical ailments that contribute to such simplistic beliefs. Again, which of us is smarter than Christ Himself? If Jesus believed in demons; it is egotistical and narcissistic to try to deny they exist.

As an avid reader, I found that the whole issue of spiritual warfare was carefully and thoughtfully portrayed in several of Frank Peretti's

---

[58] Allison, *Historical Theology*, 303.

[59] Ibid., 305.

[60] http://www.newadvent.org/fathers/2811.htm.

writings. The two most popular, *This Present Darkness* and *Piercing the Darkness*, presented an intriguing depiction of what could exist in the spiritual realm. While fictionalized, both books[61] followed in the New Testament pattern. For a lighter view of the subject, one should not overlook C. S. Lewis's book *The Screwtape Letters*.

My own experience with such issues is both personal and relational. One particular experience involved a young woman—we'll call her Betty—at a church where I served as pastor. I was approached by a close friend of Betty and was asked to visit with both of them and give my opinion as to what was going on in Betty's life. It did not take long to conclude I was in way over my head! Betty exhibited all the New Testament symptoms of demonic possession. Betty's friend and I met with Betty on several occasions praying and confronting her demon. Betty moved and ended up in a spiritual environment where she was finally able to have the demon exorcised. I ran into both Betty and her friend a few years later and found Betty to be fully recovered and leading a fruitful Christian life. While most cases of spiritual warfare I've experienced have not been so extreme or intense, Christians must realize that spiritual warfare is just as real today as in Christ's time and is just as dangerous. Satan has not given up!

---

[61] Other novels on a similar theme by Peretti include *The Oath*, *The Visitation*, and *Illusion*.

CHAPTER 10

In Conclusion

While few churches today appear to place much emphasis on spiritual issues, we must recognize that one's relationship to God and Christ is a spiritual one. We believe in what we hope for and trust in what we do not see (Heb. 1:1). This is the essence of the Christian life. Satan and his minions are constantly contending for our souls, while at the same time the Holy Spirit is the seal that protects us: "And you also were included in Christ when you heard the word of truth, the gospel of your salvation. Having believed, you were marked in him with a seal, the promised Holy Spirit, who is a deposit guaranteeing our inheritance until the redemption of those who are God's possession—to the praise of his glory" (Eph. 1:13).

When we put our trust and faith in God, we also put our trust and faith in the Holy Spirit. Unfortunately, many Christians do not understand what that means. Some don't even know there is a Holy Spirit: "While Apollos was at Corinth, Paul took the road through the interior and arrived at Ephesus. There he found some disciples and asked them, 'Did you receive the Holy Spirit when you believed?' They answered, 'No, we have not even heard that there is a Holy Spirit'" (Acts 19:1–2). Such believers live anemic Christian lives. They rely on their own strength and believe the best they can do is simply survive in this world of wickedness and deceit. They fail to reach out to others and share Christ, because they don't believe they know enough or are "saintly" enough. They fail to use their gift(s) because they don't know they even have a gift, or if they do know they have a gift, they don't know how to use it. They are content to attend church most Sundays and to throw a dollar or two into the offering; they hope this is enough to earn them a place in heaven.

On the other hand, when one truly believes he or she has received the gift of the Spirit, the person tends to become devoted to using his or her gift(s) for the good of the church. These people are not afraid or embarrassed to acknowledge their belief in Christ. One day Marge and I were climbing the "Chimneys" in the Smoky Mountains with Bob and Mary Lou Martin. While on our way down, we came across a group of teens coming up the pathway. As we passed, one of the group called out, "What do you know, man?" Without hesitation, Bob called back, "I know Jesus Christ is Lord!" Several of the group paused and then continued their climb. I've often wondered what went through their minds at Bob's remark.

I truly believe that it is God's desire that each believer grows to know the Holy Spirit and allows the Spirit to fill his or her life with all the love, peace, and joy that God intends for us. My prayer is that this little booklet will help to both inform and inspire others to become like the young couple that I got to know while serving at the Crestview Christian Church.

Gary was a nominal Christian and Connie was an atheist; both were in the military. Over time, we started having Bible study together. After about six months of Bible study, Connie decided to accept Christ as Lord and Savior and be baptized. Shortly after that, both she and Gary got out of the army and decided to return to Rhode Island, where Gary was born. They came to the church office and asked where they should look for a church when they got to Rhode Island. After referring to the *Christian Churches Directory*, I concluded they would have to look for another evangelical church, since they would be living in the middle of the state and the only Independent Christian Churches were at either end of Rhode Island. I received a phone call from a pastor in a little Baptist church about seven or eight months after Gary and Connie had left. He asked one question: "What do you do to people out there in Kansas to get them so on fire for the Lord?" He then went on to explain that when Gary and Connie started attending, the church consisted of a handful of mostly elderly people. Within three months, Gary and Connie had started a music program during worship, a youth program on Sunday night, and an evangelistic outreach program during the week. In that short time, the church doubled in size and had added several families with children. My response was simply, "We introduce them to the Holy Spirit."

May I introduce you to the Holy Spirit? If you already know the Spirit, will you introduce someone else to Him?

This is the end!

BIBLIOGRAPHY

Allison, Gregg R. *Historical Theology*. 1ˢᵗ. Grand Rapids, MI: Zondervan, 2011.

Barna, George. *The Frog in the Kettle*. Rprint Edition. Ada, Michigan: Baker Publishing Group, 1990.

Chafer, Lewis Sperry. *Systematic Theology*. Vol. VI. VIII vols. Dallas, TX: Dallas Seminary Press, 1948.

Graham, Billy. *The Holy Spirit: Activating God's Power in Your LIfe*. W. Publishing Co., 1988.

International Standard Bible Encyclopedia. IV vols. n.d.

Sinclair B, Ferguson and David F. Wright. *New Dictionary of Theology*. Edited by David F. Wright Sinclair B. Ferguson. Downers Grove, Illinios: Inter-Varsity Press, 1988.

Trench. *Synonyms of the New Testament*. n.d.

Vines Expository Dictionary of the New Testament. n.d.

Wagner, C. Peter. *Discover Your Spiritual Gifts*. Ventura, California: Regal Books, 2012.

Warren, Virgil. *What the Bible Says about Salvation*. Joplin, Missouri: College Press Publishing Company, 1982.